D0945215

THE GARDENS OF BRITAIN   3

GENERAL EDITOR: John Sales, Gardens Adviser, National Trust

Berkshire, Oxfordshire, Buckinghamshire, Bedfordshire and Hertfordshire

Richard Bisgrove

In association with the Royal Horticultural Society

B.T. Batsford Ltd, *London*

First published 1978

© Richard Bisgrove 1978

ISBN 0 7134 1178 3

Filmset by Servis Filmsetting Ltd, Manchester
Printed and bound in Great Britain by
Redwood-Burn Ltd, Trowbridge & Esher
for the publisher,
B.T. Batsford Ltd,
4 Fitzhardinge St, London W1H 0AH

Contents

List of Illustrations

(All illustrations are between pages 96 and 97)

List of Maps and Plans

List of Colour Plates

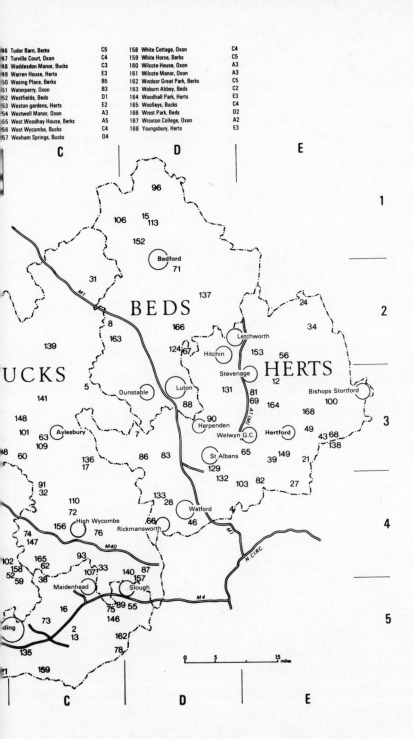

Introduction

The purpose of this volume, as of the series of which it forms a part, is to list and describe all the gardens open to the public in its area, in this case the five counties of Bedfordshire, Berkshire, Buckinghamshire, Hertfordshire and Oxfordshire.

It has not been easy to compress the descriptions of 168 gardens into a single book: some of the famous gardens in the Home Counties merit a volume to themselves and many less well-known gardens deserve lengthy descriptions to bring them to the notice of a wider audience. However, the aim throughout has been to pick out only the chief points of interest of major gardens, many of which already have substantial guidebooks, and thus to leave more space for the description of smaller gardens of particular relevance to visitors seeking ideas and inspiration for their own gardens. In all cases an attempt has been made to provide information which is not always apparent to the visitor, information on soil type, historical associations, and orientation for example, and to show how these and other factors are reflected in the design of the garden. In this way I hope the book will serve as a handbook for people visiting or planning to visit gardens, as a source of ideas for people developing their own gardens, and perhaps as a record of gardens in the 1970s which will be of some historical interest in years ahead.

Much of the information within these pages has been obtained from owners of the gardens listed, all of which have been visited in the course of preparing the manuscript and I would like to record my thanks for the time, knowledge, enthusiasm and hospitality which have every-where been freely given, underlining the feeling of kinship which exists throughout the gardening fraternity. Many of the owners of gardens spoke with pleasure of the satisfaction they receive from open-ing their gardens and of the politeness, interest and tidyness of the people who visit them. I am delighted to record here the thanks which I have been asked on several occasions to convey to garden visitors, both by owners of gardens and by the various charities which benefit from many garden open days.

Influences on the formation of gardens

The form and content of our gardens are the result of numerous
influences but one can pick out three of particular importance: historical heritage, climate and soil. All three are well demonstrated in the
Home Counties.

Historical heritage: Very briefly speaking, early gardens were small,
enclosed and formal in outline. None of these fifteenth- and sixteenth-
century gardens survive but an idea of their form can be seen in the
restored garden at Hatfield House. In the seventeenth and early
eighteenth centuries, gardens became larger, grander and more unified
in design with canals, avenues, fountains and formal features.
Chicheley Hall, Cokenach, North Mymms Park and Wrest Park
exemplify these changes in varying degrees although all have been
altered by the passage of time. Few early formal gardens survive intact
because of the eighteenth-century passion for 'improving the landscape'
which resulted in the sweeping away of formality to create extensive
landscaped parks of lakes, hills and trees. Lancelot, or 'Capability'
Brown is most well known for his works, which include Blenheim,
Hartwell and Luton Hoo but there are many other delightful parks by
lesser-known artists and by amateur 'improvers'. Buckland and Buscot,
both near Wantage, are interesting examples.

'Landscaping' was not an overnight revolution of taste. Many gardens were made in an intermediate classical style of quite formal vistas
linking architectural features and rural views. Rousham and Stowe are
internationally famous; Nuneham and St Paul's Walden Bury are less
well known but no less interesting.

Most old gardens were also affected later by the Victorian enthusiasm
for plant collecting, for elaboration and often for copying older garden
styles. Often style was superimposed on style as succeeding generations
expressed their ideals in their gardens but the nineteenth century was
notable for the great increase of population and wealth, and with these
of new houses and new gardens. There are many examples in the Home
Counties of which Ascott, Ashridge and Waddesdon are outstanding,
but the Victorian love of variety in style and content was also expressed
in smaller gardens, such as Boswells, and Sherwood (Heronsgate), both
of which are refined in character.

Enthusiasm led to excess, in reaction to which late Victorian gardens
showed a marked return to formality and firmness in design. However,
the interest in plants remained, and it is not surprising that the most
notable gardens of the early twentieth century were the combined

work of an architect, Edwin Lutyens, and a skilled artist/plantswoman, Gertrude Jekyll. Folly Farm, Sulhamstead typifies their collaboration while Checkendon Court, although the work of amateurs, remains in excellent condition as a fine example of this period of gardening splendour. The twentieth century is also undoubtedly the age of small gardens as escalating costs and shrinking fortunes cause the destruction and disappearance of large gardens. The love of plants which has characterized many ages of garden-making survives unimpaired by economic restraints but the Victorian collecting mania and the gardenesque attitude of 'plants for plants sake' is tempered as the writing of Gertrude Jekyll and the enthusiasm for flower arranging are increasingly felt. Of course it is easy to generalize and in the late twentieth century, as in any other age, there will be as many different gardens as there are gardeners. However, if it is possible to generalize at all, the modern garden is characterized by mixed planting with emphasis on foliage colours and textures and on a limited range of effect, such as grey, purple or yellow gardens in which bulbs, herbaceous plants, grasses, shrubs and even small trees are grouped to create the desired effect. Brook Cottage (Alkerton), Hill House (Stanstead Abbots) and the Old Rectory (Farnborough) are but three of several outstanding gardens of this type in the Home Counties.

Climate: Internationally, climate has had a great influence on garden styles. Indeed it has been suggested that England became a nation of gardeners because its climate is warm enough for us to be outside but not warm enough to stand still! Within the much smaller region of the Home Counties, the overall climate is not markedly varied. Rainfall increases unevenly from 22 in. a year in east Bedfordshire to 30 in. in west Oxon and south Bucks, being about 25–27 in. over most of the area. Temperatures also vary a little, influenced more by altitude than by latitude. However, the area generally is away from coastal influences and characterized by an insufficiency of rainfall in the summer months, reaching 3–4 in. deficit on average.

Much more important than regional climatic variations are changes in local climate within individual gardens. North-, south-, east- and west-facing walls or slopes and the shelter or shade derived from them have enormous influence on the range of plants which will grow successfully and there are many lessons to be learned by observant visitors. Where aspect plays a particularly important role in the design of a garden or its planting this has been pointed out in the garden description.

Weather, the day-to-day variations which add up to climate, is also vitally important in gardening. The material for this book was prepared during two very dry summers of 1975 and 1976 following the widespread floods of the 1974/75 winter. Such 'abnormal' conditions occur, albeit in less extreme forms, much more normally than we realize and the fact that the extreme drought of 1976 followed by three months of torrential rains finally added up to make an 'average year' of rainfall should be enough to warn anybody against placing too much reliance on long-term average statistics.

Of course many gardeners enjoy a challenge. Many delight in growing difficult plants and their efforts to combat the vagaries of climate by watering or covering, shading or protecting approach martyrdom. However, the evidence from visiting so many gardens in such difficult seasons emphasizes the wisdom of restricting one's choice of plants to those appropriate to the locality. What is appropriate is determined very much by the third factor to be considered, the soil type.

Soil: Whereas the climate of this area can be considered generally uniform, soil patterns are among the most varied in the country. The distribution of soils is influenced by two main factors, the geological structure of the London Basin and the effects of the last glaciers, the enormous weight of which caused the land to sink and rise as they advanced and retreated. The deposition and erosion of sediments resulting from these land movements has complicated the otherwise relatively simple pattern of outcropping in the London Basin.

The London Basin consists of a series of rocks varying in hardness and folded to form a wide, shallow trough. Sand and gravel, London clay, chalk, greensand and gault clay occupy successive layers or strata although the pattern is less clearly defined in gault clay which is interspersed with thinner deposits of greensand at its upper, more recently deposited, layers and with seams of limestone in the lower levels, merging into the great depth of limestone which underlies the whole basin. The Thames flows approximately through the middle of the central clay basin but the folding of rocks is asymmetrical, causing important scenic and soil differences. To the south the tilt is shallow and each successive layer of rock outcrops as a wide, flat, gently eroded band. To the north, the area most relevant to the Home Counties, the tilt is steeper, the outcrops narrower, less spectacular in size but more varied in character.

The clay areas, poorly drained and easily eroded, form flat plains. So heavy is the soil and so marshy the terrain that they escaped cultivation and settlement until very recent times. Now, with techniques of drainage and civil engineering greatly advanced, the clay flats near London are increasingly covered by new housing and industry but there are very few large houses or old gardens of interest on the London clay.

Sand and gravel deposits overlying the clay are totally different. These are very freely drained and very acid. Because water percolates rapidly the sands tend not to be affected by erosion but where water accumulates on less porous rocks and runs over sand, it washes away very easily to form steep hummocky hillocks with narrow valleys. Sandy areas have no agricultural value but they provide dry routes along the edge of the clay. Where sand and clay meet, springs provide an important source of water, and many landscape parks were formed on these well-watered and elevated wastelands. Otherwise the areas of sand have been left to form heaths or forests of oak, pine, birch and sweet chestnut. These cover extensive areas of Surrey, extending into Berkshire around Sunningdale and the south edge of Windsor Great Park. There is a smaller remnant westwards along the Hampshire/Berkshire border south of Newbury but similar deposits north of the Kennet have been eroded to leave only isolated spur caps. The northern outcrop also becomes confused with more recent plateau gravel deposits left by the Thames as it cut deeper into the clay. Thus the extensive gravel and sand areas of south Buckinghamshire extending into Hertfordshire are quite different in origin from the Bagshot sands although the vegetation is similar, as is their use. Many small estates with interesting houses and gardens occur in these areas.

Indeed gardens might almost be claimed to be the *raison d'être* of the settlement which has occurred. Although the soils are agriculturally worthless, they are ideal for the wide range of rhododendrons, conifers, oaks and other ornamental trees which flooded into Britain from the Far East and North America in the nineteenth century. The area around Woking, just outside our province, rapidly became the major centre for ornamental plants and the sandy areas north and south of the Thames, with their combined advantage of high, well-drained situation, natural forest and potential for garden-making, became favoured places for the rapidly increasing population of commuters to London.

Underlying the sand and clay is a great thickness of chalk which, when it outcrops at the surface, creates the characteristic landscapes of the Downs and the Chilterns. Again to the south and west, the dip of the chalk is shallow, forming wide stretches of high, undulating and open countryside, sparsely populated because of the scarcity of surface water. Formerly open sheep country, the Downs are increasingly used for cereal production. Gardens are few on this thin alkaline soil but the few that there are grow a distinctive range of plants and are often sited to take advantage of the beautiful scenery. The extensive Downs of Hampshire and Wiltshire extend just into Berkshire in a small area southwest of Newbury, rising to nearly 1,000 ft at Inkpen Beacon, with the larger area of the Lambourn Downs to the north.

The Chilterns have quite different scenery. The steeper dip of the chalk has been eroded into smaller, irregular hills and the great depth of eroded chalk has left thick deposits of clay with flints to cap each hill. The clay is often acid, thickly wooded and, with the combination of scenery and proximity to London, the area is quite densely populated.

Below the chalk is greensand, easily eroded and important in its own right only when it occurs in flat beds, south of the London Basin. To the north it occurs as isolated outcrops (in the Harcourt Arboretum of Oxford Botanic Garden for example) and as an admixture with gault clay, producing quite fertile soils. To the east the outcrop is more pronounced forming a ridge of sand through Bedfordshire from Linslade and Woburn to Sandy, with wider tracts forming Thetford Chase in Norfolk.

Deep gault clay outcrops over much of central Oxfordshire, north Buckinghamshire and Bedfordshire. It is poorly drained, flat and sparsely settled except for towns of the brick-making belt. However, the clay is interspersed with seams of limestone, the presence of which is very important in Oxfordshire and Buckinghamshire. Along the north edge of the Downs and Chilterns the springline has resulted in the settlement of many small villages. Between this line and the minor outcrop of limestone from Faringdon to Oxford is the Vale of the White Horse, both margins of which have many interesting, often small, gardens on the fertile soil which results from the merging of clay and limestone. The valley cut by the upper Thames separates the first low ridge from the deeper seam of limestone forming the Cotswolds. Fertile soil, numerous small streams and plentiful building stone have resulted in an area of many small and exceedingly beautiful villages. The area is high and exposed, but golden stone walls shelter many an interesting garden.

In Buckinghamshire the limestone is less important, with the exception of the low ridge on which Aylesbury stands above an otherwise extensive clay plain. North Buckinghamshire lies under boulder clay, left by the retreating glaciers. This is a mixture of sand, clay and stones, more fertile than the massive gault. At the northern edge of the county the Ouse has cut through clay to expose limestone in a shallow limestone valley giving rise to a further series of small towns and villages between Buckingham, Newport Pagnell and Bedford.

The plants: The geological structure which has so much determined the patterns of settlement, agriculture and natural vegetation has also had its effect on gardens. The clay belts are not much settled but widespread oak forests have contributed centuries of accumulated leaf-mould and abundant surface water allows the cultivation of woodland plants and waterside plants where gardens are made. In more open situations, where forest has long since disappeared, the heavy clay supports flourishing modern roses.

The meeting of clay and lime results in more fertile soils. Rhododendrons and their numerous allies fail without special nurture, but roses, and rosaceous plants (*Cotoneaster, Malus, Prunus, Sorbus*), many other shrubs and herbaceous plants flourish. On lighter limestone soils, bulbs and hellebores flourish and many gardens are open early in the year. On the lightest soils, spring flowers are even more important and carpets of snowdrop, anemone, aconite and narcissus beneath still leafless beech create beautiful effects. Tender plants can also be grown in sheltered corners and the great range of herbs and grey-leaved plants flourish in open situations. Such is the effect of clay and lime that one can almost construct a geological map by comparing the distribution of gardens open in April, for narcissus and cherries, and June for roses.

Where drainage is due to sand rather than chalk, quite different plants are seen. Roses, other than *Rosa rugosa* and a few other species, disappear but the vast range of *Ericaceae* (heathers, rhododendrons, *Pieris, Kalmia*) and trees for autumn colour come into their own. Many of these plants grow well, although slowly, where the sand is deep, but houses and gardens occur more often where clay is not far below the surface, and where sand or gravel overlie clay, the moist soil and abundant springs offer limitless opportunities for gardening.

The gardens: The effect of soil types on the range of plants and on the quality of lawns lends an unmistakable, if subtle, regional character to gardens but the most important influence on a garden is its owner. It is particularly interesting to compare groups of gardens near one another to see how much variation is possible even when using many of the same plants, as often happens when gardeners in a village exchange plants among themselves.

The range of gardens in this volume is enormous, ranging in size from a few square yards to many acres, in soil from pure sand to heavy clay and in age from three years to 300. Indeed, although about 200 gardens are listed, no two are alike. The condition of gardens also varies. Extremes of weather or the temporary loss of a gardener can create temporary setbacks in any garden but it is sad to record the general air of despondency among owners of large gardens. Death duties, crippling taxation and the escalating costs of wages and materials have caused many people to reduce their staff until, in some instances, grass-cutting is the only regular care which the garden receives. Even major houses and gardens which we take for granted as part of our national heritage can not survive indefinitely in such an adverse situation. After seeing the satisfaction which gardeners derive from their work compared with factory workers, and seeing garden staffs reduced within a few decades from 10, 20 or 30 gardeners to one or two while unemployment and a general mood of dissatisfaction gains momentum, one wonders if the attempt to even out wealth is entirely beneficial.

The situation in rather smaller gardens, of two to five acres, is more encouraging. Here the activities of an enthusiastic owner can make a world of difference and there are several new and thriving gardens of this size in the Home Counties. Also of interest is the willingness of owners of several small gardens to open their gardens together. This is especially helpful in showing the variety which can be achieved within the general constraints of soil and climate, and in offering ideas and inspiration to those in the process of making their own gardens.

Arrangement of the list of gardens: All the gardens are listed in a single, alphabetical list. Groups of gardens are listed under the village in which they are situated and the naming is such that up-to-date information on opening times may easily be found from the annual lists mentioned below. Thus the Manor Houses in Bampton and Milton are listed under 'Bampton' and 'Milton', whereas those in Bledlow, Sutton Courtenay and elsewhere are listed as 'Manor House, Bledlow' etc., simply because this is the way in which they are listed in annual indices.

Other categorization has been deliberately avoided. Even arrangement by county is not wholly satisfactory as boundaries have changed recently enough to cause confusion and there are many gardens situated in one county but with the nearest town, from which directions would be given, in the adjacent county. Gardens of particular historical or botanical interest are sufficiently described in text that no further categorization is required, nor is a symbol used to denote gardens suitable for wheelchairs. Many gardens cannot be traversed entirely in a wheelchair but, where views or accessible parts of the garden are particularly good it would be unfortunate to deter visitors. Also, so much depends on the person in or behind the wheelchair. Much of my decision to omit symbols derives from having led a group of severely disabled garden enthusiasts around a garden noted for its steps, terraces and other hazards. It involved some effort to negotiate obstacles but the satisfaction expressed by the party was worth every effort. Where particular problems may arise, these are again mentioned in text and further indications may be obtained from annual lists of open gardens.

The one distinction which is made is between 'amateur' and 'professional' garden opening. The division is not hard and fast but many gardens open only infrequently and the proceeds go to charities. Several owners of such gardens expressed the desire to remain anonymous so no names are given. Other gardens are open more frequently, or have corporate owners. In the former case the proceeds will be used to maintain and develop the garden and, in both cases, the ownership is indicated.

It is clearly not possible to give exact dates of opening or costs of entry, which vary each year, but the frequency and season of opening are indicated, together with the source from which current information can be obtained. The information was up-to-date when prepared, but gardens may cease to open at short notice, so intending visitors are earnestly requested to check in annual lists for current opening arrangements and not to arrive at other times. The sources mentioned are as follows:

GS: The Gardeners' Sunday Organization, White Witches, Claygate Road, Dorking, Surrey. *Gardens to Visit* lists gardens open in support of The Gardeners' Royal Benevolent Society and The Royal Gardeners' Orphans Fund.

HHCG: *Historic Houses, Castles and Gardens*, ABC Travel Guides Ltd, Oldhill, London Road, Dunstable, Beds. A list of gardens etc. open frequently, including National Trust properties. Details of National Trust opening arrangements are also sent annually to Trust members.

NGS: The National Gardens Scheme, 57 Lower Belgrave Street, London SW1W 0LR. *Gardens of England and Wales* lists gardens open in support of The Queen's Nursing Institute and the National Trust.

RC: British Red Cross Society, 9 Grosvenor Crescent, London SW1X 7EJ. *Open Gardens Guide* lists gardens open in support of the Red Cross.

The first three publications are available each spring from most booksellers. The Red Cross list may be obtained from County Red Cross headquarters or from the address above, for a small charge.

Adwell House, Tetsworth, Oxon

5 acres; 1 gardener; clay soil. Open one weekend in June for NGS. 4 miles S of Thame; ½ mile S of A40 between Tetsworth and Postcombe.

This fifteenth-century house has a dignified eighteenth-century front looking onto rose borders against the hedge which screens the house from the drive. At the side of the house the paved floor of a demolished conservatory offers a home for herbs and associated plants. There is also a small rose garden near the swimming pool. The secluded walled garden near the chapel has several interesting climbers and a lily pond. The main feature, however, is the lawn with its fine specimen trees, many planted early in the nineteenth century by the owner's great-grandmother. Others have been planted more recently to ensure a continued succession. The lawn and walled garden slope down towards a canal and cascade with groups of waterside plants in the thicker woodland.

A trout fishery has been developed from the streams and springs which abound on the estate, and the chain of ponds created in recent years is being incorporated into the garden.

Allanbay Park, Binfield, Berks

8 acres plus fields, lake and woods; 2 gardeners; gravelly loam changing to clay in the field below. Open once in May and July for NGS. 8 miles E of Reading. 2 miles N of Binfield on B3018 (Binfield–Twyford).

Allanbay Park has a long, very narrow garden of many parts, strung along the boundary of an open meadow with a lake. It has been rescued from a state of complete dereliction since World War II.

To the south is a ride through woodland of red oak with rhododendrons, azaleas and primulas bordering the path. A colonnade erected in 1950 marks the end of the garden proper but the ride continues to a secluded seat overlooking the lake. In 1971–2 the tennis court was converted to a rose garden, with a swimming pool separated from it by a rose hedge. Roses on chains loop along the boundary for 250 yards, past the house to a second, smaller rose garden east of the house and along the flower garden beyond.

The kitchen garden north of the house is very irregular in shape, having been developed from an old farmyard, but the box-edged paths meander to establish something of the quartered pattern traditional in walled gardens. The narrow area between the kitchen garden and field boundary is developed as a flower garden with a secluded summerhouse. Large curved borders against the wall were designed by Lanning Roper in 1974 and include many grey-leaved plants among the herbaceous plants for effect and ease of maintenance.

A long walk with newly-planted shrubs in grass leads past the orchard to the northern extremity of the garden. This square enclosure includes the tip of the lake, here narrowing to a winding stream. A mount in the grove of trees is topped by a wrought-iron domed rotunda, a classical scene in minature and a delightful terminus to the garden.

Appleton House, Appleton, Oxon

2 acres; part-time gardener; limestone soil. Open once in June or July for NGS. 5 miles NW of Abingdon. Turn N off A420 (Oxford–Swindon). House in centre of village behind war memorial.

The main garden is south of the former rectory, within a circular stone wall. Its curve is echoed by raised borders of iris and grey-leaved plants with a deeper rose-terrace facing west. The lawn is shaded by four trees: walnut, *Catalpa*, *Robinia* and a large *Liriodendron* planted *c.*1880. The wall does not completely enclose the garden, but re-curves west of the house forming an entrance to the rectangular north garden. The garden in general is planted for all seasons with bulbs, hellebores, roses and climbers, thriving on this alkaline, retentive soil. The wall provides sheltered or shady borders in which different plants flourish.

A door in the east wall, by a border of nerines, opens into the kitchen garden. Here, stone garden buildings and walls loosely divide the area into several compartments, and a pergola of fruit and flowering climbers spans the main path. This path connects the courtyard on the south to the orchard on the north. Beyond the old yews of a hedge which once terminated the garden, roses and flowering trees have recently been planted.

Arkley Manor, West Barnet, Herts

8 acres; 6 student gardeners plus 3 staff; gravel over London clay. Open twice each May, June, July, Sept. for GS, NGS and Good Gardeners' Association. 2 miles W of Barnet on Rowley Green Road, ½ mile N A1, A411 junction.

Arkley Manor is the Headquarters of The Good Gardeners' Association and a training centre where six or seven students from all parts of the world are taught organic gardening. The garden was set out in 1960 by the well-known author W.E. Shewell-Cooper to demonstrate the advantages of organic gardening. There is no digging or forking done in the garden: a small rotary cultivator produces the necessary tilth for seed-sowing in the vegetable garden. Elsewhere a one inch mulch of compost or sedge peat all over the soil suppresses weeds and produces an excellent soil structure, even on the very thin gravelly soil over London clay.

Like many demonstration gardens, Arkley Manor consists of many differing areas but it is impressive for its range of demonstrations. There are shrubs and ground-covers, herbs and herbaceous plants, collections of ferns, irises, *Hemerocallis* and heaths etc. and a large rose garden. These flower gardens are grouped around the lawn south and west of the house.

Beyond the flower gardens are plantations of many soft fruits and top fruits, all grown in grass or under straw mulch and trained to demonstrate the various methods of pruning. Also in this area are the large vegetable garden, a range of different types of glasshouses, cut-flower beds, borders of newly introduced annuals, a collection of weeping trees and, of course, the large compost bins around which the activities of the garden revolve.

A guide is available, most plants are labelled and the bookshop sells a wide range of books and pamphlets by Dr W.E. Shewell-Cooper in aid of The Good Gardeners' Association, a registered charity.

Ascott, Wing, Bucks
(The National Trust)

30 acres; 8 gardeners; calcerous gault clay. Open April–Sept.: Wed, Sat and Bank Hol Mon 2–6; also Sun in July. Aug see HHCG. Open one Sunday in each month April–July for GS. NGS.

Ascott, part of Baron Mayer de Rothschild's Mentmore Estate, was used as a hunting box by his nephew Leopold from 1874. The original seventeenth-century farmhouse was soon lost within the long, half-timbered structure of the present house. Simultaneously the gardens were made by the Veitch nurseries under the personal supervision of Sir Harry Veitch, who was probably also responsible for the design. The gardens were complete by 1900 with many evergreens for interest in the winter, when the house was most used.

From the forecourt a grass vista extends between the kitchen garden and a newer cherry orchard to an oval lily pool, also used in the past for ice-skating. The main garden, however, is south of the house. Although in many ways a typical Victorian garden it is unusual in its arrangement, having open grass terraces below the house and enclosed formal gardens on the perimeter, quite the reverse of the normal situation in which formal gardens around the house open onto more spacious lawns, orchards or parkland.

The terraces, from which there are distant views of the Chilterns across the Vale of Aylesbury, end above 'The Madeira Walk', where tender wall shrubs are trained against the south-facing retaining wall. Across the walk, lined with colourful bedding plants, is a circular garden with a large circular pool and a splendid statue of Venus in a shell chariot, the work of the American sculptor Julian Story. At the east end of the terraces is a sundial garden with the central gnomon, numerals and surrounding motto clipped in box and yew. To the west, paths meander down the slope across tre-scattered lawns. The upper path ends on the top of a grotto above the Dutch Garden, a formal garden of circular flower beds and a tiered fountain (also by Sorty) arranged along a tapering vista between high clipped hedges. Below the Dutch Garden, the path continues through a rock garden to the 1897 Jubilee Plantation in the south-west corner.

Although the garden was completed by 1900 it did not, of course, cease to develop. When Anthony de Rothschild inherited the property he planted large numbers of flowering cherries in the orchard north of the house and in a delightful dell west of the Dutch Garden. Bulbs are freely naturalized throughout the garden with narcissus and fritillaries spreading as they might in the wild. After World War II the neglected aster borders and herbaceous borders against the east hedge of the Dutch Garden were grassed over. Tufa was taken from the rock garden, also overgrown, to make a fernery on the unwanted tennis court above the sundial garden.

Mr and Mrs Anthony de Rothschild gave Ascott to the National Trust in 1949. Since then vigorous shrubs have been established to separate the drive and south garden, making the garden more of an entity. Most recently, in 1976, the herbaceous borders were reinstated to add yet another feature to this fine garden.

Ashdown House, Ashbury, Oxon (The National Trust)

40 acres; maintained by farm staff and (hedges etc.) by contractors; soil derived from varied glacial deposits over chalk. Open April, Wed only; May–Sept, Wed, 1st and 3rd Sat of month, 2–6. See HHCG. On W side of B4000 between Ashbury (2½ miles) and Lambourn (3½ miles).

From a narrow road high in an apparently deserted valley of the Lambourn Downs, the sudden appearance of Ashdown House is a surprise and a delight. Built c.1650 of chalk with stone quoins, the four-storey house stands stiffly elegant, topped by a golden-crowned cupola from which there are magnificent views.

Traces of a formal layout remain in the west lime avenue (naturalized with snowdrops) and in an old lime walk around the woodland, but the setting is generally of grass scattered with large stones deposited by glaciers. In contrast to the openness of the surroundings there is an intricate parterre on the west side of the house. Designed by A.H. Brookholding-Jones and planted by the National Trust c.1956, the pattern is attractive when viewed from the house, but doubly attractive when seen with the trim lines of the house as a background. The north lime avenue was planted in 1970.

The house was built by the 1st Lord Craven for Elizabeth of Bohemia and given to the National Trust in 1956, with 40 acres of the park, by Cornelia, Countess of Craven.

Ashridge, Berkhamsted, Herts (Ashridge Management College)

90 acres; 7 gardeners; acid, clay over chalk. Open April–Oct: Sat, Sun and Bank Hols, 2–4. (House open only 13 days each year, see HHCG.) 3½ miles N of Berkhamsted, 1 mile S of Little Gaddesden.

The thirteenth-century monastery at Ashridge became a royal palace in the sixteenth century after its appropriation in 1535 by Henry VIII, but it is with the nineteenth century and Humphry Repton that Ashridge is particularly associated.

From 1808 to 1814 the house was rebuilt by James Wyatt for the 7th Earl of Bridgewater and the enormous gothic house remains as a fantastic backdrop to the garden. Repton was consulted about the gardens in 1813 and Ashridge was one of his last, largest and most significant commissions, for he departed from broad landscape designs to design a series of small, formal gardens, much influenced in their themes by romantic associations with the former monastery. As with many Repton schemes, his ideas were not followed exactly: the Countess of Bridgewater and her head gardener, Hemmings, improvised on Repton's plan, and additions have continued to the present day.

The 90 acres of garden lie mainly south of the house, within the 3,500-acre Ashridge estate owned by the National Trust.

Near the east end of the house is the orangery (now converted into bedrooms), approximately on the site of the Jacobean house. The large yews were probably part of the seventeenth-century garden but the Italian Garden with its central fountain is c.1900 in origin. A more complex design than the present one can sometimes be discerned in the grass during exceptionally dry weather. From the south terrace, bright with bedding among clipped yews, there is an open vista between scattered trees on the left (including an oak reputed to have been

ASHRIDGE

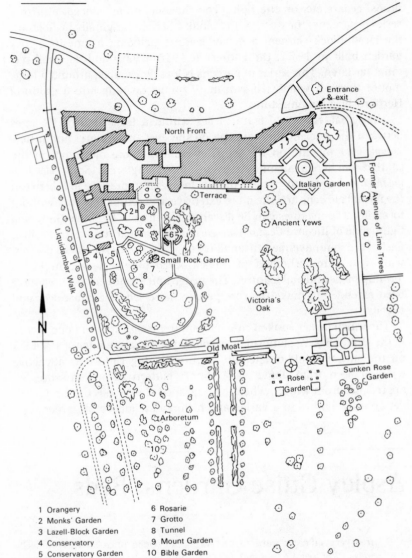

1 Orangery
2 Monks' Garden
3 Lazell-Block Garden
4 Conservatory
5 Conservatory Garden
6 Rosarie
7 Grotto
8 Tunnel
9 Mount Garden
10 Bible Garden

planted by Princess Victoria in 1823) and thicker groups of rhododendrons, cedars etc. on the right. The rhododendrons conceal a further series of gardens: the Rosarie and Monk's Garden (originally by Repton); the Lazell-Block Garden, a newer feature including a limestone rock garden built in 1973; the Fernery (*c.*1910–1920) and its small rectangular lawn. This series of gardens is loosely grouped around a large mount through which winds a flinty tunnel opening into a grotto of Hertfordshire puddingstone.

This great variety of features lies within a level area of 15 acres between the ancient lime avenue on the east (now gone) and a new *Liquidambar* avenue on the west, extending to the old moat on the south. From here a magnificent avenue of Wellingtonias (*Sequoiadendron giganteum*) lined with rhododendrons forms an impressive link between the formal gardens and the more extensive arboretum, itself not without formality. Old avenues can be discerned, leading to the Bible Garden, a tight circle of Incense Cedar (*Calocedrus decurrens*) around a stone bible. East of the main avenue is a small rose garden (formerly a herb garden) with twin 'summerhouses' of clipped beech (one replanted in 1975) forming most unusual features. The hedge and fencing in this area have been extended to make the rose garden more secure against deer and rabbits.

The much larger sunken rose garden to the east, forming one corner of the main 15-acre platform, was constructed in the winter of 1974/75 on the site of a mid-nineteenth-century skating rink. It is attractive whether seen from above as a simple pattern of modern roses or appreciated from within, when the fragrance of roses fills the air. It adds yet another feature to a varied and historically important garden.

Aspley Guise Gardens, Beds

Three very different gardens on pure sand. Open once in May for NGS. 2 miles W of exit 13 from M1 on B557 (towards Bletchley). *Aspley House* is east of the village, on B557; *Manor Close* and *The Rookery* are near the church N of the village centre.

Aspley House (5 acres; no gardener): Although very much simplified to keep maintenance within the abilities of its busy owners, there is still much of historical interest at Aspley House. In 1958–62, the main formal vista, obliterated by eighteenth-century landscaping, was re-established. The original drive had survived so well that it was possible to plant new beech hedges with the same slight taper that had been used on the drive to create a false perspective. West of the new, curving drive are more recent shrub plantings around a small clearing. This area is shaded by several fine old trees, although several more have succumbed to age.

North of the house, rising ground and enclosing walls prevented extensive vistas. Instead the central panel was terraced in the early 1960s to balance the house.

On either side, behind *Thuja* and yew hedges, were the kitchen gardens. The west side still produces vegetables in a steeply sloping walled garden with a young orchard at the top and, tucked by the house below, a small paved garden of great charm. On the east side, a swimming pool has been installed, necessitating more terracing but opening up an informal glade among the large trees and wall shrubs of the garden below.

Manor Close (2 acres; part-time gardener): Manor Close was built in 1969 to take advantage of the best part of the Manor House garden, which the owners relinquished after developing it from a ruin in 1930. The entrance, skirting open fields with distant views between new clumps of trees is in contrast to the intimacy of the garden itself. A border of rhododendrons and other shrubs along the drive is recessed along the hedgerow to create a miniature glade of bulbs and small trees north of the drive. On the south side is a small orchard and vegetable garden.

The secluded west garden, behind the house, is only ¼ acre in extent but has many lessons for cramming quarts into pint pots. A brick-paved terrace is divided from the lawn by a low hedge, with a much taller Lawson's Cypress hedge flanking handsome Italian gates to divide the lawn from the walled rose garden. The bold scale of the gates and the clever recessing of the hedges creates a sense of spaciousness which is assisted by the careful reliance on balance rather than symmetry. The curved border of roses and herbaceous plants to the left of the gates is not mirrored but is balanced by a tiny, low-walled spring garden and pool to the right. The brick terrace, open by the drawing room, narrows to a path between more roses, a little garden in itself, before turning among irises along the north side of the house to return to the drive.

The Rookery (5 acres; 1 gardener): Although by modern standards a large garden, land form has been used to great advantage to create a variety of small sheltered corners with an expanding background of woodland. The Victorian façade of the house, complete with conservatory, looks out over a small level lawn enclosed by roses on one hand and a steep mixed border on the other. (This lawn, incidentally, demonstrates convincingly what can be achieved by regular applications of peat and fertilizer even on very poor sandy soil.) The view continues over a small valley to the high opposing bank clothed with rhododendrons.

Starting below the lawn the valley forms a grassy walk winding in a long spiral around three sides of the hill. The south side is a wide, shady dell with the trees carefully thinned and underplanted; on the west it climbs along the side of the hill between a bank of brooms and the steep-sided bowl of an old sandpit, and by the time it turns north, the path occupies an eminence above a beech plantation established in 1955, with glimpses of a second part of the garden below. The summit of the hill is a small lawn with a horseshoe flower garden above the house.

It is the necessary to descend through the little cut-flower garden, to the lower garden. This large, flat grass area is divided by a wide border of buddleias and roses. In addition to a new vegetable plot there is more ornamental planting around the tennis court, backed by the steep slope of the sandpit already seen from above. This slope, formerly covered with elm, was replanted in 1974 with beech, birch, ash and *Rhododendron ponticum*.

Bampton Manor, Bampton, Oxon

4 acres; 2 gardeners; gravelly loam over limestone. Open once in April, June and Aug for NGS; also open Wed and Fri afternoons for sale of plants. At entrance to Bampton on Witney–Faringdon road (A4095).

Bampton Manor garden has many features of varying character, but all have in common firm outlines and good colour combinations of many interesting plants. It is, as a result, interesting throughout the year.

Although an old garden, most of the planting has taken place since 1948, much of it more recently as a result of the loss of large trees. At the entrance, this loss has allowed the development of a long pool surrounded by shrubs to conceal the drive. Across the drive, the circular white garden enclosed by yew hedges is also new. The trees west of this white garden were planted in 1976 to replace an elm avenue which crossed the garden nearby.

The drive winds between these features to the south front of the house where wisteria, *Nerine,* prostrate rosemary and other sun-loving plants flourish. At either end of the south front are secluded formal gardens. To the east a garden of herbs, 'Ballerina' roses, grey-leaved plants and bright verbenas opens into a shaded walk. Tall shrubs concealing the back drive have been underplanted with still more interesting plants. To the west the plan is more simple but the house, steps, loggia and walls are wreathed in trailing and climbing plants, a luxuriance which continues into the adjacent swimming pool garden.

From the south front itself, a vista extends between iris borders edged with lavender, pleached limes underplanted with Crown Imperials, deep herbaceous borders backed by yew hedges and, finally, informal banks of shrub roses before terminating in a wide screen of shrubs and trees. West of this vista and below the walls of the kitchen garden is an informal corner shaded by beech and sycamore. Here bulbs and winter flowering plants are planted in long drifts to provide colour before the canopy develops overhead.

Within the two walled gardens old box hedges and wall fruit remain but the borders are increasingly used to raise plants for sale.

Barry's Close, Long Crendon, Bucks

2 acres; 1 gardener; clay soil. Open once in June for NGS. 2 miles N of Thame, on B4011 (Thame–Bicester) at lower end of Long Crendon village.

Barry's Close is not an old house. It was made by converting farm buildings in 1925/6 and the oldest-looking part was in fact added subsequently, in 1935, thus enclosing a yard which, with old apple trees and a border of cottage plants, has much old world charm.

The main garden, west of the house, is more open, sloping down gently from the terrace to a water garden then rising steeply to the boundary. The water garden has a series of small spring-fed pools among large rocks clothed in potentillas, heathers, maples and other shrubs. The steep grassy bank is planted with a great variety of young trees and shrubs, with a few of greater age including the rare *Rhus verniciflua,* the Japanese Lacquer Tree.

On the north boundary is a summerhouse against a flourishing rose bank, designed and planted by John Mattock and Sons. Roses grow, too, at the top of the slope, where *Rosa filipes* 'Kiftsgate' scrambles over a dead plum tree, but this very sheltered corner is now being devoted to more tender plants.

From this corner a path leads up to the vegetable garden, quite separate from the main garden. Returning to the house, festoons of ivy decorate the north-facing wall of the house, the loggia and the nearby fence to provide permanent interest.

Barton Abbey, Steeple Aston, Oxon

10 acres incl. 3-acre lake; 2 gardeners; clay loam. Open one Sunday in May and August for GS, NGS. 12 miles N Oxford. From A423 turn W on to B4030 at Hopcroft Holt Hotel. After ¾ mile, turn left.

Although old, the garden at Barton Abbey continued to develop until after World War II. To the south of the main drive is a lake surrounded by large trees and grassy slopes, thickly planted with daffodils. Around the lake there are thatched playhouses, a splendid arch of whalebone and a bridge leading to overgrown paths through a woodland garden, beautifully constructed but now almost lost in undergrowth. Many shrubs can still be appreciated, however, from below and from the path above, leading to the tennis court. A swimming pool nestles in a small sheltered hollow near the house and above it a rose garden picks up the formal lines of the house.

On the north side of the drive are the stables, a two-acre kitchen garden and a tiny enclosed spring garden now quite overshadowed by the large *Parrotia* and *Cercidiphyllum* within it. The stables house a Shetland Pony stud and other horses which are a great attraction on open days. Although the surroundings of the kitchen gardens are now neglected, the greenhouses still contain peaches and grapes, beautifully trained and in a condition seldom seen elsewhere.

Benington Lordship, Benington, Herts

7 acres; 1 gardener; clay over chalk. Open one weekend in June for NGS. 5 miles E of Stevenage midway between Walkern (on B1037) and Watton-at-Stone (on A602).

Even in neglect this was an interesting garden, but if the improvements begun in recent years are continued, it will become a remarkable garden indeed. The house was built in 1740 adjacent to a Norman keep, which doubtless inspired the elaborate Victorian folly adjoining the east side of the house. The garden was developed mainly after 1918 for the grandfather of the present owner by the former's brother-in-law.

The ruined keep was planted as a winter garden, and many winter-flowering or evergreen plants remain. Adjacent is a rose terrace. To the west, both terrace and house overlook two small lakes below the steep grassy slope.

The main path traverses the top and bottom of the slope by two very different routes. The upper path, just below the house and rose garden, descends steeply to a small box-edged lawn overhung by tall ever-greens. A central statue of Shylock marks the crossing of the north-south axis by a long flight of steps forming a vista to the uppermost end of the lakes. The lower path meanders along the lake edge to open suddenly into a large rock garden which merges gradually from the horizontal waters of its pools to the vertical Lawson's Cypress effectively screening the garden.

Both walks continue across the garden but the lower one, through the rock garden and orchard, arrives at the lowest point of the double herbaceous border, from which position it is most spectacular. The borders rise between the walled garden on the left and shrubs and conifers on the right. Above the walled garden, bricks give way to pleached limes, the path curves below the new swimming pool garden and returns towards the house.

Since 1973 the present owners have rescued the garden. Borders and rock garden are being replenished with interesting plants but the rescue proceeds cautiously for fear of destroying the maturity and mystery to which the garden still owes much of its charm.

Billingbear House, Binfield, Berks

5 acres; 1 gardener; gravelly loam. Open once in June for GS. 3 miles NW of Bracknell. 1 mile N of Binfield from B3018 (Binfield–Twyford) turn W for Billingbear House ($\frac{1}{4}$ mile).

The drive to Billingbear House passes among large oaks east of the kitchen garden to a large forecourt north of the house. The large kitchen garden is, perhaps, the most interesting part of the garden despite its simplification. The two original walled enclosures have been combined and the east part is now orchard with a tennis court and swimming pool against the end (west-facing) wall. A central wellhead and pergola remain from a more elaborate layout. The west part remains productive with greenhouses, fruit cage and vegetables. One path retains the charming arches of trained apples, and it is worth visiting the north corner to see the old wall with its heating flues.

The 'L' shape of the kitchen garden and the curve of the drive are dictated by a remnant of the old moat, around which has developed a pleasure garden with borders of herbaceous plants and roses against the walls, azaleas and lilacs in the grass and low shrubs along the moat itself. The intimacy here is in contrast to the open character south of the house.

A wide terrace scattered with self-sown lavender has an enormous wisteria dominating other wall plants. Below the terrace, a fine Manna Ash (*Fraxinus ornus*), twin Blue Cedars and a small rose garden are the only features on an otherwise open lawn allowing uninterrupted views across the ha-ha to the countryside beyond.

Blenheim Park, Woodstock, Oxon (His Grace the Duke of Marlborough)

60 acres pleasure garden (8 gardeners) and 8-acre kitchen garden (4 gardeners) in 2,000-acre park; gravel soil. Open late March–Oct, 11.30–5.0 every day. Garden centre. (For palace opening see HHCG.) In Woodstock, 8 miles N of Oxford on A34 (Oxford–Stratford).

Blenheim may justly claim to be one of the oldest and greatest gardens in England. When Henry II lived at Woodstock Manor, a few hundred yards from the present palace, he created an idyllic retreat for his lover, Rosamond Clifford, around a spring gushing from the hillside nearby. Rosamond's Well remains although the manor-house was demolished during the building of Blenheim.

Queen Anne granted the Manor to the Duke of Marlborough after his victory at Blenheim, and Sir John Vanbrugh created the great palace, the bridge and the fortress-like walls which encompassed the garden. For the walls of the kitchen garden alone, at an angle to the main axis to provide two south-facing walls, half a million bricks were used. Henry Wise, Queen Anne's gardener, was responsible for the garden itself. From June 1705 fleets of barges and wagons brought plants from the Brompton Park nursery of London and Wise, and by October the 75 acres of manicured neatness was complete. Large elm trees were brought in to make the avenues, and, by 1707, Wise reported with delight that only 30 of the 1,600 elms had died. The Duchess's garden was filled with a great variety of flowers; in the kitchen garden there were vines, peaches, figs and pears of the best sorts, while apples, mulberies, cherries and quinces grew in the orchard to the south, making the finest kitchen garden in England. Despite changed circumstances, the kitchen garden remains an impressive reminder of the great formal garden.

Alas Marlborough fell from favour. He left England in 1711 and work on the garden ceased. He died in 1722 but Sarah, Duchess of Marlborough, continued to make improvements: the Column of Victory and the Triumphal Arch by which visitors enter the park illustrate the heroic scale which Sarah considered necessary to commemorate her husband's achievements for his country.

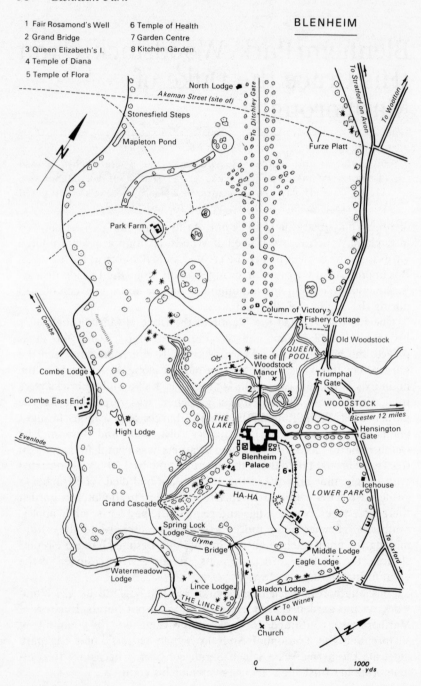

1 Fair Rosamond's Well
2 Grand Bridge
3 Queen Elizabeth's I.
4 Temple of Diana
5 Temple of Flora
6 Temple of Health
7 Garden Centre
8 Kitchen Garden

BLENHEIM

After her death in 1744 Blenheim suffered neglect and, from 1758, deliberate destruction as the 4th Duke laid out the garden in the new picturesque manner. Many architectural features were added, and Lancelot Brown was employed from 1764. Although he is remembered unfavourably for his destruction of the great parterres in favour of 'grass to the very door', it was his construction of the foaming cascade south of the palace which created the two great lakes welding the palace, the bridge and the park into a unified composition.

The 5th Duke succeeded in 1817. His passion for collecting, which had kept him near to bankruptcy for much of his life, was unabated. At Blenheim he determined to make the finest botanical garden in Britain, with the newest and rarest plants interspersed between rustic bridges, grottoes, fountains and cottages, especially in the area below the cascade. Many of the trees remain but the intimate landscape is now a true wilderness. Other features were added throughout the nineteenth century but it was the 9th Duke (1892–1934) who made the greatest changes and reinstated some of the original grandeur.

From 1895 to 1919 nearly half a million trees were planted. The elm avenues were restored and oaks planted enough 'for 500 years to come'. The Great Court was repaved, having been grassed by Brown. The Italian Garden, with its scrollwork of box accentuated by pots of flowers, was designed by Achille Duchêne for the site of the 1st Duchess's garden and, from 1925–30, Duchêne continued with the water terraces which are now such an important feature. The rock garden started by the 5th Duke beyond the cascade was developed anew and, although it is now overgrown and concealed from distant view, it remains an interesting feature for the explorer.

The 10th Duke also added to the garden. From 1954 soil was imported from Bladon Heath to establish the rhododendrons, pieris and other shrubs which line the grassy walks south east of the palace, along the edge of the original parterre.

Despite the recent ravages of Dutch elm disease and a succession of very dry summers, large numbers of newly planted and well-maintained trees in the park indicate the continued interest of the present Duke. He has also developed the garden centre and other attractions to increase revenues and thus ensure the continued survival of this great garden.

Bletsoe Castle, Bletsoe, Beds

3 acres; part-time help; clay soil. Open once in June for NGS. $6\frac{1}{2}$ miles N of Bedford. From A6 turn E at Bletsoe sign near 'Falcon Arms', then $\frac{1}{4}$ mile. House near church.

Although a very old house, Bletsoe Castle had no garden until 1965, when the present owners arrived. A moat surrounds three sides of the garden within a boundary wall, so the potential for garden development is considerable.

To the east is a walled kitchen garden, on a slope sufficiently steep to allow views over the high wall. To the north and west the moat is shaded by tall trees and, although extremes of weather have made the water level most unpredictable, a start has been made here on a water garden. The main garden, though, is on the open lawn to the south.

Between the moat and boundary wall is a new yew hedge beyond which are many shrubs and trees for autumn colour. These will provide an increasingly attractive background to the garden, replacing the many elms which have been felled. The moat itself has been partly filled in so the depression is now shallow enough to admit rose borders and a sheltered paved garden against the fifteenth-century bridge which spanned the moat. A new border has also been established against the wall which separates the lawn from the drive.

Throughout the garden the emphasis is on freedom of growth, on the mixing of plants of all kinds to create pleasing associations of foliage or flower and on creating interest throughout the year. Although the garden is still quite young, the wisdom of these policies is already apparent.

Borlases, Waltham St Lawrence, Berks

6 acres; part-time gardener; clay soil over chalk. Open one Wed in late May, June, Sept and Oct. 7 miles E of Reading on B3024 (Twyford–Windsor), 300 yds W of memorial cross.

The garden at Borlases was designed *c.*1918 around a much-enlarged Tudor farmhouse by Capt. Davidson with help from Gertrude Jekyll. Although neglected from 1939 to 1966, it has been gradually restored since then, retaining many interesting features and plants.

The most unusual plant is *Umbellularia californica*, planted as a tender wall shrub but now grown into a wide-spreading and handsome ever-green tree, much to the disadvantage of the adjacent wall. Its distinctive appearance, something between a bay and evergreen oak, is more than equalled by the aroma of its crushed leaves. It is important both for its rarity and for its key position between the open lawn with large oaks to the west of the house and the more intimate gardens to the north.

A pergola divides the north garden. To the east, enclosed by beech hedges is the summerhouse overlooking herbaceous borders and an old herb garden. The deep border into which the summerhouse nestles is penetrated by a narrow, winding brick path. To the west, the garden is more open with vistas loosely defined by Pfitzer Junipers and plant beds. *Acer pseudoplatanus* 'Brilliantissimum' turns the axis between borders of 'Iceberg' roses and old azaleas towards the spring-fed lily pond, once a farm pond, and thus back to the main lawn.

Boswells, Wendover, Bucks

12 acres; 2 gardeners; thin chalk soil. Open twice in June for NGS. On E side of A413, 1 mile S of Wendover.

The house and garden at Boswells were begun in 1901 in open fields, the garden being much enriched after 1929. It is a Victorian garden in the best sense, with a few quite narrow bands of planting dividing the garden into several varied and interesting parts.

The drive climbs between close rows of beech planted in 1910 and (with *Berberis x stenophylla* beneath) in 1925–29. A bend and dense shrub belt mark the concealed entrance to a partially walled and very productive vegetable garden while, across the drive, the path leads through overgrown shrubs to a secluded tennis court and small formal garden almost engulfed in *Paeonia lutea, Sorbaria* and *Osmanthus.* A turn in the path leads to a deeply shaded border of *Hosta* and *Astrantia* then, by contrast, to the open forecourt. The drive itself continues along the margin of an open lawn before entering the walled forecourt draped in still more interesting shrubs.

From the garden front of the house a loggia opens onto a semicircle of lawn from which three wooded vistas radiate, recalling views of Gertrude Jekyll's house 'Munstead Wood'. At Boswells the 'woodland' is only a few plants deep but includes a large Judas Tree, *Cercis siliquastrum.* The main vista quickly opens onto a double mixed border backed by yew hedges. Cross-walks open onto two lawns, one enclosed by a nut walk, the other open to reveal extensive views. Both lawns have Deodar Cedars (planted in 1906) and the latter, larger lawn also has a cut-leaved beech and the handsome *Aesculus indica.* Beyond the chestnut the lawn returns to a more formal area of shallow terraces and hence to the forecourt or, passing a huge *Garrya elliptica* on the corner of the house, to the semicircular lawn.

In common with many larger gardens parts of Boswells have been virtually abandoned but much of it remains in excellent condition. It is of great interest for its design and its many unusual plants often grown to enormous size.

Brook Cottage, Alkerton, Oxon

---

3 acres; 1 gardener; heavy loam over limestone. Open two weekends in May/June and July for NGS. Also by appt. 6 miles W of Banbury. From A422 (Banbury–Stratford) turn W to Alkerton.

This is undoubtedly one of the most interesting gardens in the Home Counties, planted with an excellent sense of colour association, a feeling for the linking of building with garden and an obvious love of plants and gardening. It began in 1964 but much of it is more recent than this. The steep west-facing hillside has resulted in the development of four long gardens side by side up the hill, a difficult garden for visitors in wheelchairs but with help to negotiate one or two flights of steps there is a great deal to be seen in the more level parts of the garden.

The 'L' shaped house and a barn (now a studio) form a shaded court festooned with climbers: the combination of *Hydrangea petiolaris* and *Tropaeolum speciosum* is especially good. There is a short steep climb to the top of the garden where a new stone wall (1973) is already clothed with interesting shrubs, then a gradual descent between long islands of planting to join the second path.

This begins on a small lawn by the studio. On the left is the bank of shrubs already seen from above and on the right is a hedge of *Senecio* 'Sunshine' which extends the length of the main garden. The hedge is allowed to flower before being cut back, forming a ribbon of yellow out to a large yellow border which is a key feature of the garden. The yellow border, one of the oldest plantings, was substantially revised in 1975 and contains both yellow or yellow/green foliage (fennel, ivy, *Euphorbia*) and yellow flowers (*Hypericum*, roses, *Potentilla*).

The third axis, continuing from the drive, is the most formal and is terraced. From the drive a gate opens into a paved court, the south- and west-facing walls and freely draining borders of which have been used to grow many exciting tender plants. Millstones and slim cypress punctuate the opposite side. The purple and blue colour scheme is very effective. A large rose bed and broad flight of steps lead down to the main lawn, the downhill edge of which is firmly edged in yew. On the opposite bank a variety of shrubs has been planted through polythene sheet held in place by crazy paving, for weed-suppression. This lawn ends with perhaps the best full view of the yellow border.

The fourth way through the garden is the newest. Informal stone steps descend to a sloping lawn and the raised borders of a white garden begun in 1974. With an abundance of fast-growing grey-leaved and white-flowered plants it was effective even in its first year. A golden *Catalpa* in the lawn, at present still a small shrublet, introduces the yellow garden of golden hollies and other bright foliage which will eventually cover the steeper slope.

From this point all paths converge at a small pool nestling in the bank, its banks and water surface lushly planted. Beyond it is the second part of the garden, around the tennis court. The scale of planting here is larger and in a few years it will form an impressive backcloth for the brighter colours of the flower garden.

Spirals of copper beech enclose a circular garden with a central spire of *Picea omorika* and for more temporary effect, *Salix purpurea* 'Pendula', toning beautifully with the beech. Viburnums supporting *texensis* hybrid clematis clothe the nearby tennis court bank. At the further end willows and Leyland Cypress have been planted for rapid effect. The upper bank has many good foliage shrubs while the end of the tennis court accommodates a group of old species and modern shrub roses.

In 1974 the paddock beyond the tennis court was taken into the garden and the two ridges planted with seedlings of many *Sorbus* and maple species. Losses in the dry summer of 1975 were heavy but the effect of tree groups and glades, merging the garden with its surroundings, will slowly gain in stature while the more transient schemes around the house are experimented with and redeveloped.

Broughton Castle, Banbury, Oxon (The Lord Saye and Sele)

3 acres; 1 gardener; fertile loam over ironstone. Open Weds, April–Sept; Suns June–Aug, and Bank Hol Mons, 2–5. Parties by appointment at other times. See HHCG. 2½ miles SW of Banbury on B4035 (Banbury–Shipston-on-Stour).

Broughton Castle was built in 1306 and enlarged at the end of the sixteenth century. The symmetrical north front looks across an open courtyard to the gatehouse which guards the moated island. The south front, with its great variety of windows and carved stone indicates the long history of the building.

The garden, dating from the late nineteenth century, comes as a surprise, concealed by a high curtain wall from the courtyard. It was in part the work of Gertrude Jekyll and, although the extent of her involvement is unknown, her influence remains apparent in the long colour borders. The garden was almost entirely replanted in 1968.

A rampart walk, now inaccessible, has been colonized by white valerian among which new roses climb. The long walk, along the west side of the house, is edged by box on one side and by flourishing borders against the walls on the other. To the north, the border is of bright blue, yellow and white flowers in contrast to the south border of softer pink and silver. Before one reaches the pink border, however, the main feature of the garden is suddenly revealed.

Within the walls of the old kitchens and yard is a beautifully maintained knot of box-edged fleurs-de-lys and circles, filled with pink roses,
grey *Teucrium* and lavender. *Fremontodendron californicum* and *Eucalyptus gunnii* thrive in sheltered corners, while by the old water-hole is a
shapely Japanese Maple. The sundial surround was, until recent, the
coping of a pool in the adjacent formal garden, but this has been swept
away to leave a single, wide border of shrub roses and herbaceous
plants. A handsome arch at the end of the border spans a path along the
moat, back to the long borders.

Broughton Poggs and Filkins Gardens, Oxon

Several gardens on limestone; open once in April and Sept for NGS.
Broughton Poggs and Filkins are Cotswold villages between Burford and
Lechlade, just E of A361.

The gardens are all more-or-less flat but are otherwise varied in size and
character. They include:

Broughton Rectory (1 acre; 1 gardener): This approximately square
garden has its house in the centre of the plot. The vegetable garden is
screened within the curve of the drive by a dense shrub border. On the
other three sides of the house are open lawns, connected by straight
gravel walks and edged by a long mixed border around the entire
boundary. A narrower border against the house is filled with sun-
loving plants while behind the house a rose-covered walk extends
between wide flower borders to provide a more intimate, shaded
character. The design is simple and very satisfying.

Cotswold ($\frac{1}{10}$ acre): In contrast to larger gardens in Filkins, 'Cotswold' is
a perfect cottage garden. Owned by a retired stonemason who con-
tinues to carve in stone and wood, the garden is bright with spring and
summer bedding near the roadside, with a tiny and sheltered 'succulent
mosaic'. Trained fruit and vegetables occupy most of the space away
from the road and a small greenhouse is used to raise most of the plants
for the garden.

Abbeystones ($\frac{1}{4}$ acre): The bungalow and garden are both designed and
maintained by the owner who is confined to a wheelchair. On a narrow

triangular plot, the bungalow and garage occupy the wide end with a small lawn at the narrow end and a fine mixed border along the whole of the long side. Grey-leaved plants, low shrubs, roses, bulbs and herbaceous plants combine to create a long season of interest while reducing maintenance to manageable proportions.

Little Peacocks ($\frac{1}{2}$ acre; occasional help): Owned by one of Britain's most distinguished landscape architects, Little Peacocks shows garden design of the most subtle and charming quality. The house, outbuildings and office are grouped around the drive and with a walled vegetable garden and small 'front garden', occupy about half the plot.

The remaining half, along two sides of the square, has a meandering lawn bordered by an intimate mixture of ground-covering plants beneath pears and a young horse chestnut for height and shade. In one corner, grey and purple foliage predominate, in another hellebores and spring bulbs; behind the office are plants for deep shade, but nowhere is there a hard and fast division between groups. Spring bulbs, autumn cyclamen and *Colchicum* in large numbers, *Hosta*, ferns and many other plants, common and uncommon, are used not as specimens but to form a variety of interrelated spaces.

St Peter's House (1 acre plus rough grass): Designed in 1936 by Brenda Colvin, this garden retains the clean lines and clear distinction between heavily planted borders, open lawns and rough grass which contribute to ease of maintenance. It is, nevertheless, a varied and interesting garden. The drive is enframed by alternate plant groups. To the right a herb border and espalier fruit conceal the vegetable garden; to the left a dense shrub border conceals the boundary and to the right again a shrub group at the corner of the house divides the short 'back drive' from the forecourt. The forecourt and lawn of complementary shapes are fringed by rough grass and bulbs with trees for autumn colour, and by a low mixed border terminating at a sheltered seat.

A path through the border leads to a second lawn and hence to a sunken paved garden now almost immersed in cushions of crevice plants. The size of lawns, borders and other features is nowhere large, but they are so well related and shaped that the garden seems much larger than its single acre.

Broxbourne Gardens, Herts

Two adjoining gardens with gravel soil over clay. Open once in May for NGS. 5 miles SE of Hertford. From A10 in Broxbourne, turn up Bell Lane or Park Lane into Baas Lane.

Baas Cottage ($\frac{1}{2}$ acre; 1 day a week help): Built in 1965 in a corner of the next garden, Baas Cottage appears a large house on this $\frac{1}{2}$ acre triangular site but its placement in the centre of the north side of the plot has left space on three sides. This space has been used with much skill to create a varied and interesting garden.

The drive curves around a cherry tree, shaping a border which is filled with plants for all-year-round effectiveness. Heathers and good foliage shrubs are displayed against golden *Robinia* 'Frisia' and *Cupressus macrocarpa* 'Lutea', and a blue form of Lawson's Cypress, particularly attractive with festoons of *Tropaeolum speciosum* scrambling through it. On the north side of the house is a diminutive but productive vegetable garden.

The south side is shaded by birch and beech, under which are established islands of rhododendrons, *Hebe*, hydrangeas and, by a spring-fed ditch, many waterside plants to emphasize the woodland character.

The top border wraps around an open lawn at the west end, from a small greenhouse to the shade garden, with a backdrop of trees in the next garden. This is a well-stocked mixed border with tall roses, recuperating camellias from the house, paeonies, penstemons and many other plants including a *Ceanothus impressus* grown to become a small tree!

Hipkins (3 acres; 1$\frac{1}{2}$ gardeners): This attractive tile-hung house was built in the 1930s and the garden, developed mainly after the war, was enclosed from open fields. Now it is surrounded by new houses but the attempt to retain a quiet country outlook has succeeded to an astonishing degree. A narrow belt of willows, birch, hollies and rhododendrons is carefully pruned to maintain a 'woodland' fringe which will not overshadow the garden. In the west corner, behind one of several spring-fed pools, the screen is deep enough to admit winding walks with views back to the house. Elsewhere, close inspection reveals houses only a few yards away.

The short entrance drive curves between the orchard and a copse of birch, through which there are delightful views of the garden, to a heavily enclosed forecourt. Bright colour is concentrated for effect, immediately around the house, around the pool which forms such a feature in the garden, and near the birch copse as an eye-catcher. This concentration emphasizes the quiet greenness elsewhere in the garden.

East of the house is the vegetable garden, enclosed by hedges. The central path leads into a group of new mountain ash which reinforces the screen of birch and beech separating Hipkins from Baas Cottage.

Bruern Abbey, Churchill, Oxon

10 acres; 2 gardeners (with a further 2 acres and 2 gardeners in the nursery); clay soil. Open once in April for NGS. 5 miles N of Burford between A361 (to Chipping Norton) and A424 (to Stow-on-the-Wold).

Bruern has a long history and the garden is, as a result, a charming blend of formal and informal features. Birds and wild flowers are encouraged wherever possible, not least around the fish ponds east of the house, remnants of a Cistercian monastery now softened in outline. In contrast, the main approach west of the house has been restored to pristine formality with pleached limes planted along the wide gravel approaches in 1952/3. To complete the renovation, old Portugal Laurels lining the west approach are being replaced by young clipped hollies. In 1972/3 a large Victorian extension was demolished and the seventeenth-century roadside buildings were reconnected to the main house (of *c*.1720) by new wings to create a paved court, furnished in summer with orange trees and other tender plants.

From the south front the terrace, with its carefully concealed swimming pool, descends between twin borders (planned by Lanning Roper in 1960) to the main vista, an eighteenth-century yew avenue now interplanted with amelanchier. The vista extends over a lily pond, with varied crab apples to soften and frame the vista.

Between this strong formal axis and the older carp ponds are more intimate areas. A *Robinia* avenue and hornbeam hedge, planted in 1954, surround the tennis court and rose garden, a delightful corner, designed by John Fowler in 1955. More varied and informal trees, including a group of white-stemmed *Betula ermanii* are interspersed with play equipment.

Across the road is the topiary nursery where 10,000 hollies in 16 varieties are established. The wide main path with new arches of trained apples and wisteria combine the charm of an old kitchen garden with access for modern tractors.

Buckland, near Faringdon, Oxon

30 acres, inc. 6-acre lake; no gardener; Cotswold rag soil on high ground, Oxford clay in valley. Open once in April for NGS. 4 miles NE Faringdon, $\frac{1}{2}$ mile N of A420 in centre of village.

Buckland is a beautiful self-contained village of Cotswold stone. The old crafts of stone masonry, thatching and joinery are still much in evidence as may be seen by the fine condition of the garden buildings. The garden is of historical rather than horticultural interest: an English landscape garden with strategically placed focal points around a serpentine chain of lakes. It was created as a setting for Buckland House (built by the younger John Wood of Bath in 1745) by Richard Wood, a pupil of 'Capability' Brown.

From the old Manor House, now encrusted in Strawberry Hill 'gothick', a yew-lined walk descends to the ice-house, from which the first glimpse of the lakes is obtained. Below the ice-house, open grassy areas alternate with dark tunnels of yew to reveal views of the ice-house, rotunda and exedra.

The grass is strewn with flowers, native and naturalized, and fine trees punctuate the scene between the bridge (1820) at the lower end of the lakes and the eighteenth-century exedra (rebuilt in 1976) at the upper end. The large cut-leaved beech is particularly impressive.

From the exedra the path rises through the deer park to the rotunda and into the shade of large Wellingtonias, cedars and other ever-greens around the entrance to Buckland House. A chestnut avenue leads to the house itself and continues back to the Manor House, passing the terrace of Buckland House, from which the landscape can best be seen in its entirety.

Burloes, Royston, Herts

3 acres plus woodland; part-time gardener; thin chalk soil. Open once in late July or August for GS. 1 mile E of Royston on S side of A505 (Royston–Newmarket).

In 1900 this high, exposed site on the northern edge of the chalk offered fine views but was not the most auspicious site on which to develop a garden. However, extensive beech woods were planted, a house built and the slope gently terraced. Today the formal garden lies in a sheltered amphitheatre between the house and wings of woodland looking over the same unspoiled view, now diversified by groups of trees in the parkland. The house was rebuilt in 1937 after a disastrous fire.

A beech avenue climbs to the forecourt, whence a vista through the woods extends along the ridge of the hill. Beech, as a hedge, also separates the forecourt and the garden below. Shallow terraces descend from the grey borders along the south-east front of the house to the rose garden and hence to an open lawn with fine views. The vista is enclosed by yew hedges backing twin borders of shrubs and iris. To the northeast the hedge opens onto a shaded lawn beneath tall beech and cedar. On the south-west side the hedge is double, enclosing three smaller gardens. The uppermost has yellow and white borders, distinct but harmonious in their colouring; the central garden is of paeonies and silver-leaved pear, but the lower borders have been replaced by cut flowers and vegetables.

In complete contrast to this formality south east of the house, openings to the south west lead to an informal glade on the edge of the woods and thus to a long ride cut through the woodland itself.

The grouping of house, stables and enclosing woodlands, the balance of formality with informality and the contrast of elegant vistas with interesting borders gives Burloes an air of maturity which belies its twentieth-century origins.

Buscot Park, Faringdon, Oxon (The National Trust)

85-acre garden in 3,800-acre estate; 4 gardeners; clay-loam. Open April–Sept, Weds and first complete weekend in each month, 2–6; Oct–March, Weds only, 3–6. See HHCG. Open once or twice annually for GS, NGS. See also *Old Parsonage, Buscot*. On A417 between Lechlade (2½ miles) and Faringdon (3½ miles).

Buscot House is an old house in a relatively new setting. The first known house on the site was built *c*.1775 for Edward Loveden Townsend. It is likely that Townsend himself was the designer of the house, and of the park, with its two lakes, to the north east and north west. West of the house, approached through the elegant stable-block, is a series of walled kitchen gardens, five acres in total, with the central octagonal garden being the largest. A third lake, above the kitchen gardens, is a nineteenth-century addition.

In 1885 Buscot Park was acquired by Alexander Henderson, later Lord Faringdon. He enlarged the house and began the formal garden with Harold Peto as architect. Peto was a leading figure in Italian Renaissance revival and his main work at Buscot, the long water garden, is very Italian in character. Constructed between 1905 and 1910 it linked the house and the main 20-acre lake to the north east. Peto also designed the forecourt, since modified, and the wide terrace to the north, from which both lakes can be seen.

From 1931 the 2nd Lord Faringdon reduced the house to its original central block with pavilions to east and west. The west pavilion contains servants' quarters. The east pavilion, housing a squash court and theatre, spans the axis over the sunken swimming pool, and across the grassy slope to a low balustrade. This overlooks a 'patte d'oie' of three avenues of Fastigiate Oak, ordinary Pedunculate Oak, beech and poplar, linked by cross-axes in a complex pattern. The irregular compartments thus formed have been planted with a variety of trees: Purple and Weeping Beech, Indian Bean Trees, small flowering trees and tall conifers of varying ages.

The west garden is much less complex. A new sycamore avenue has replaced the dead elms along the drive. This crosses the smaller lake and passes through a pinetum to the forecourt, from the south-west corner of which steep flights of steps descend between yew hedges to the main axis of the kitchen garden already described.

The house and 55 acres were given to the National Trust by Mr E.E. Cook in 1948 and the remainder of the estate was acquired under his will in 1956. It is let to Lord Faringdon.

Bussock Mayne, Snelsmore Common, Berks

9 acres; 3 gardeners in summer, $1\frac{1}{4}$ in winter; soil varied, from gravel cap over clay. Open once in May, once in July for NGS. 3 miles N of Newbury on B4494 (Newbury–Wantage) S of M4 bridge.

The garden of Bussock Mayne is on undulating ground west and south of the house, with farm buildings to the east and an open grassy approach on the north. In 1946/7 H. Milner-White designed the approaches, the rose garden and kitchen garden, conveniently near to the house but well screened from it. Subsequently A.J. Ivens (of Hillier and Sons) became an advisor and friend, resulting in the planting of many unusual trees and shrubs, one of the rarest being the large, evergreen *Lyonothamnus floribundus aspleniifolius* by the loggia. In 1947/8 the rock garden was made, rock being one of the few things not rationed after the war! Designed by the owner and constructed by Pulhams, well known for their work at Chelsea and Wisley, it begins at the old pond below the rose garden, and follows a small natural valley, well screened from the house. With the planting of the orchard above the rock garden in 1949/50, the aim of concealing the boundary from view was achieved.

In 1960/62, the house was doubled in size and a large swimming pool made in a sheltered hollow west of the rock garden. The dense shrubs above the pool and grove of varied and interesting trees on a more distant spur are now established sufficiently to create bold masses framing distant views. Broad grass rides between these major features merge the garden into the surrounding countryside.

High on the west side of the garden is a grassy terraced walk among the trees. The central hollow fills with water in the winter forming a pleasant canal, but it dries more or less completely in the summer to leave an elevated, secluded walk from which to appreciate the garden and its rural surroundings.

Capel Manor Institute of Horticulture, Waltham Cross, Herts (London Borough of Enfield Education Committee)

7 acres plus 23 acres paddock etc; 6 gardeners; clay soil. Open one weekend each month April–Sept, excluding August. Horticultural groups by appointment. 2 miles N of Enfield. From Cambridge road (A10) turn W into Bullsmoor Lane. Entrance on right.

Capel House was built in 1793 and renamed Capel Manor after the demolition of the nearby manor-house. In 1840 it was purchased by James Warren who planted many of the fine trees to be found in the garden. The last private owner, Colonel Medcalf, was very interested in horses and built the handsome stable block: the plentiful supply of manure from the stables has considerably assisted the development of the new garden. After Medcalf's death the estate was leased and later purchased by the London Borough of Enfield and, since 1968, has served as a centre for horticultural education. Most of the new planting has been done since 1971.

A teaching garden is a most difficult garden to design but Capel Manor has managed to overcome the conflict between collecting and displaying plants: the variety of situations in the old garden has been well exploited to create a wide range of luxuriant schemes which are a great credit to the small and enthusiastic staff. The basic philosophy has been to group plants harmoniously in appropriate settings, with a spontaneity and informality which is also reflected in the courses offered. Each part of the garden leads naturally to the next and although most parts have one well-defined season of interest, carefully chosen supporting planting ensures that the garden as a whole is always attractive.

The walled garden east of the house has several glasshouses ranging

from old lean-to vineries to a modern aluminium alloy widespan structure. These are variously adapted for propagation, teaching and display,
including a stove house, alpine house, a landscaped warm-temperate
house and small units to suggest how amateurs (including those
physically disabled) may make the best use of their own greenhouses.
The glass is clustered at the east end of the walled garden, while a
diagonal pergola with a range of interesting climbers leads from the
main entrance to the centre of the western half, which is heavily
planted and very attractive. Roses are the main feature, with borders of
old and modern shrub roses to illustrate the development and use of our
most important flower. One corner has been designed and planted as an
amateur's garden by groups of students and the walls have wide
borders around their base. The south-facing border is filled with doubt-
fully hardy plants. A splendid mixed border occupies the whole length
of the south wall, about 200 feet, and despite its north aspect it is well
furnished with roses, clematis, sub-shrubs and herbaceous plants
spilling onto the path.

Outside the walls the mood changes. Here the north-facing border is
heavily shaded, wet and has been heavily over-limed in the past. The
range of plants flourishing in this inhospitable situation offers inspiration to anyone planting a shaded town garden. This border leads to an
equally shaded nuttery in which the hazels have been thinned and
underplanted to create a delightful spring garden of bulbs, hellebores
and early flowering shrubs. A tall *Liriodendron* marks the end of the
spring garden and the path emerges onto the open lawn near the
house. The Copper Beech, one of the first planted in the country, about
1760, is the tallest in the country.

The fringe of trees enclosing the lawn has been carefully thinned,
underplanted and developed as a woodland walk. Long accumulation
of leaf litter has acidified the soil and made possible the planting of early
rhododendrons and tender Chilean shrubs which benefit from the
shelter and light shade.

At the north end of the lawn, large island beds of species roses have
been established with a background of newly planted trees and shrubs
for autumn fruit and foliage. This smaller planting leads naturally to
the rock garden of Macclesfield quartzite, built from 1969 to 1971
around two sides of the old pond. The steep banks, the easy transition
from open lawn to undulating heathers and bold grouping of rock
contribute much to the success of this area.

From the rock garden a straight walk leads alongside the demonstration area in the north-east corner back to the walled garden. The
demonstration area is not without attraction but its main object is more

purposeful. It includes a new herb garden, annual borders, a hedge collection and a paved area designed particularly for disabled gardeners. Plots demonstrate the effects of pH, weedkillers and fertilizers on various plants and a glasshouse is at hand for use as a classroom in wet weather.

Chandlers Cross Gardens, Rickmansworth, Herts

Four gardens on acid gravel soil over chalk. Open once in September for RC. Chandlers Cross is $2\frac{1}{2}$ miles N of Rickmansworth–Watford road from Croxley Green; 2 miles W of A41 (Watford–Hemel Hempstead) from Huntonbridge.

Chandlers Farm (3 acres; 1 gardener): The short drive leads to a spacious circular drive with the old façade of the house, wreathed in wisteria and grape, on one side and a long barn on another. Behind the barn is a maze of small, productive vegetable gardens. On the other side of the drive a curving terrace leads to a rose garden backed by shrubs, then past newer extensions of the house to the swimming pool and the main lawn.

The layout around the lawn is intricate, with the shrub borders sheared to keep them in bounds, but there is considerable variety of planting. The manicured parts of the garden are adequately balanced by the surrounding orchard and rough grass areas for children's play.

Penmans, Penmans Green (2 acres; part-time gardener): This garden has been simplified but the effect remains satisfying. The drive is made roughly circular by curving beds of roses and dahlias around a central willow with a bank of scattered small trees (many of them birthday presents!) on one edge. A double herbaceous border runs along the end of a productive vegetable garden: the stables at the end of the garden have contributed substantially to soil fertility.

The drive, borders and vegetable garden occupy rather more than a half of the width of the plot. The narrower remainder has the house itself (with a tiny conservatory crammed with plants) and a lawn on two levels. The upper part, fringed with trees, ends with a Copper Beech and pairs of cedar and redwood flanking the slope to the lower lawn, formerly a tennis court.

White House (4 acres; 1½ gardeners): The garden here was once more elaborate than the other three and is mainly a spring garden. The house is late Georgian and was extended in 1880 at which time much of the garden was designed. The drive curves round to the forecourt, bordered by rhododendrons which conceal the flower garden. This is intriguingly developed with winding paths, rockwork, and a wealth of rhododendrons, maples, witch hazels and other plants which thrive on this light acid soil. The convolutions of the path lead finally to a handsome pergola opposite the south end of the house and thus to a wellhead backed by a buttressed yew hedge.

Although much of the intricate rockwork is now overgrown, simplification elsewhere has improved the garden. Half the kitchen garden has been swept away and grassed giving a more pleasing vista from the terrace and ensuring that the reduced vegetable garden with its borders of fruit trees can be managed more satisfactorily.

In addition to the garden, on the open day there is an exhibition of paintings by local artists in the gallery.

Yew Court Farm (2 acres; 1 gardener): The entrance to Yew Court Farm can have few equals. An arch through an old barn by the roadside (now a garage and picture gallery) leads into a courtyard fringed with buildings on three sides, their deep tile roofs sweeping down. The courtyard is bright with flowers and the fourth side of the court has a low wall separating it from the swimming pool garden where borders curve back to reveal views across the ha-ha.

A side gate by the pool opens to the back yard with its chicken house, outbuildings and vegetable garden, and thus onto the second lawn. The house (*c.*1720) was skilfully enlarged in 1965 and the old front entrance, wreathed in roses, is now a charming sunken terrace. From here one looks across the lawn to a shrub border backed by large rhododendrons, and a group of yews which gave the farm its name. Rhododendrons and yews flank a deep herbaceous border screening an old tennis court, now planted with fruit trees.

Chastleton House, Moreton in Marsh, Oxon

1 acre remnant of large garden; no gardener; limestone soil. Open week-days (except Weds) 10.30–1; 2–5.30; Sundays 2–5. Closes dusk in winter. See HHCG. 4 miles SE Moreton in Marsh, 5 miles NW Chipping Norton, off A44.

Chastleton House was built in 1603 and the garden designed *c*.1700 but the latter has largely disappeared. There are, however, two topiary gardens, much renewed over the years, to round off a visit to the most interesting house.

West of the house the lines of a terrace and square plots of an early garden are easily discernable and in the centre is a beautifully clipped circle of yew within which are concealed 24 yew shapes, some now very abstract!

The malthouse garden, in which teas are served in summer, is more elaborate in its arcaded surround of yew and has a beautifully trimmed hedge topped with birds against the road, but its most interesting feature, is a yew 'millstone' in low relief.

Checkendon Court, Checkendon, Oxon

7 acres plus woods; 2 gardeners; sandy soil over chalk. Open once in May and August for GS or NGS. In triangle between Henley-on-Thames (7 miles), Reading (8 miles) and Wallingford (7 miles). Entrance next to Checkendon parish church.

Although the house is partly Elizabethan, the garden of Checkendon Court dates almost entirely from *c*.1920 when the then owners, Mr and Mrs F.S. Oliver, restored the house and designed its Edwardian sur-roundings.

The drive, bordered by Irish Yews, emerges from woodland to the forecourt and extensive open lawns, across which hedges of box and yew, beech and holly create formal vistas. A slight bank in the north corner of the lawn outlines the original Elizabethan bowling green.

From this north-east garden an opening by the tennis court leads to the vegetable garden, planned on the same bold scale. A heavy door at the south-east end of the house opens into a more intimate sunken garden. The charming portico overlooking this garden, added by the Olivers, opens into a small paved garden and hence onto the lawn. A sunken swimming-pool garden, an informal orchard and small ornamental trees surround the lawn and soften rather than conceal the yew hedges which are so important in the design. These double hedges contain herbaceous borders and also give the setting an interest which it would lack if laid open to full view. From an octagonal pavilion outside the hedge this wider view can be enjoyed.

A small azalea garden terminating the double borders marks the crossing of two major vistas, one continuing into the adjacent woodland, the other through the vegetable garden. The main path and cross walks of the vegetable garden are also lined by double borders in which roses, herbaceous plants, dahlias and annuals are carefully arranged. The garden has escaped the grassing down of borders which has destroyed so many fine Edwardian gardens and although the woodland walks which extend from the several cross paths have suffered from reduced maintenance, the natural effect of rhododendrons and lilies growing along the paths through increasingly natural woodland serves to highlight the character of the garden proper.

Chicheley Hall, Newport Pagnell, Bucks (The Hon. Nicholas Beatty)

15 acres; 2½ gardeners; clay soil. Open April–Sept, Wed, Thurs, Sat, Sun and Bank Hols, 2.30–6. Parties any time by appt. See HHCG. S of A422 between Newport Pagnell (2 miles) and Bedford (11 miles).

Chicheley Hall was built in 1719–23 for Sir John Chester by Francis Smith of Warwick, and displays artistry and craftsmanship of a high order. Setbacks in the family fortunes protected the house and garden from later fashionable alterations. Charles Bridgeman was consulted in 1725 but Sir John Chester died within months so the plans never materialized and Chicheley remains a rare surviving example of a complete country house and garden.

Sir John succeeded to the estate in 1698 and immediately began improvements – elm, horse chestnut and lime avenues were planted by 1701 and an elm avenue in 1714. The present lime avenue is more recent. In 1700–1701 George London was paid for his work on the canal but whether London made the canal or merely filled in one side of an older moat is not clear. The presence of ancient fish ponds below the canal make the latter suggestion a distinct possibility.

The house itself came rather later. The stables were begun in 1716, the house followed, and the service wing was completed in 1725. As the steep slope prevented the grouping of buildings around a court they are arranged almost in a line with the south forecourt enclosed between the stables and a wall. A wide walk along the east front of the house leads to a secluded north garden with a single wide border along its south-facing wall.

Below the main walk is a wide platform of grass enclosed on three sides by London's canal. Parterres below the ramp have long since disappeared but some old Holm Oaks and Cedars remain from the formal layout. Beyond the canal, which has recently been cleaned and restored, are the old fish ponds and banks of daffodils.

The cobbled west court has low-walled enclosures opening from it. These have been developed in recent years as the kitchen garden with a newer pleasure garden opposite the north wing.

Church End, Bledlow, Bucks

$\frac{1}{5}$ acre; no gardener; thin chalk soil. Open *by appt only* May–August inclusive for NGS. 1$\frac{1}{2}$ miles W of Princes Risborough, $\frac{1}{2}$ mile off B4009 opposite church.

Gardens open only by appointment tend to be small but richly planted, and this one is no exception. Begun in 1958, the garden conveys a great sense of distance in a small rectangular plot.

The front garden is surrounded by high banks of shrubs which conceal the drive. The garage is submerged beneath *Vitis coignetiae* (as is a neighbour's garage by a cutting from this plant) and the north side of the house peeps from a blanket of *Osmanthus delavayi* and hydrangeas, climbing and shrubby. The topiary peacock is a recent addition.

At the back of the house is a tiny paved suntrap. Although most of the garden is on a north-facing slope, this corner has been raised behind low drystone walls creating a sunnier aspect and a deeper peat-enriched soil for alpines. Informal steps lead to an elliptical lawn surrounded by shrub roses and hence through an arch to the irregularly shaped upper lawn shaded by seven closely planted trees. Two of these shelter a spreading *Viburnum plicatum* and herbaceous plants to create a woodland walk in miniature. An old mirror brings light into the darkest corner of the garden and its reflections give the impression of a glade continuing into the distance. The reality of a neighbour's garage behind the mirror is discernable only at very close range! Another walk leads along a climber-clad fence to a small utility area.

The whole garden is planted with a great variety of paeonies, hellebores, lilies and other interesting plants.

Cliveden, Taplow, Bucks (The National Trust)

180 acres (plus 250 acres woodland); 9 gardeners; chalk with acid gravel pockets. Garden open Mar–Nov, Wed–Sun and Bank Hols, 11–6.30. (House open Apr–Oct, Wed, Sat and Sun, 2.30–5.30.) See HHCG. 3 miles N of Maidenhead. From A4, ½ mile E of Maidenhead bridge, turn N through Taplow on B476. Entrance opposite 'The Feathers' inn.

Cliveden is a superb site developed by a series of very wealthy owners over a span of three centuries. George Villiers, 2nd Duke of Buckingham, purchased Cliveden on his return with Charles II from exile in Italy and France. In 1666 he began to build on high ground with panoramic views over the Thames. His great redbrick terrace establishing the different levels of the north forecourt and south lawn, remains as the basis of the present house. A sword and the date 1668 marked out in flower beds east of the house commemorates his elopement with the Countess of Shrewsbury. Alterations and additions to the house continued for most of the Duke's life. After his fatal riding accident in 1687

Lord George Hamilton (later Lord Orkney) bought the house and, in 1735, employed Giacomo Leoni to build an octagonal temple and the Blenheim Pavilion. These were probably intended, with the recently restored amphitheatre, as elements in a new landscape garden.

From 1739 to 1751, Frederick, Prince of Wales, leased the house, and in 1747 the *Quercus ilex* grove was planted, reputedly by his surgeon. Lancelot Brown was consulted in 1777, probably for minor alterations to an already well-developed scheme. As a result of eighteenth-century plantings, the open panorama admired by Evelyn in 1679 is now enclosed by magnificently wooded slopes.

In May 1795 the house was destroyed by fire. It was rebuilt in 1824 but burned again in 1849, soon after its purchase by the Duke of Sutherland. In 1850/51 the Duke commissioned Sir Charles Barry to design the third house to stand on the old terrace. From 1852–55 John Fleming was appointed head gardener. He created the great parterre in 1853/54 and it has been suggested that it was he who began the idea of successional bedding schemes so immensely popular in late Victorian times. Queen Victoria was herself a frequent visitor, and the Green Drive was used to shorten her carriage ride from Taplow Station.

With the building of the clock tower and stable block in 1860/61 the forecourt took on its present form. In 1893 the property was purchased by William Waldorf Astor (later 1st Viscount Astor) who established many of the garden features seen today.

Cliveden was given to the National Trust in 1942 by the 2nd Lord Astor but the family remained for many years. From 1969 it became the English campus of Stanford University. Although the gardens are much visited, most visitors remain in the environs of the house and miss the many features in more distant parts of the grounds.

The main drive from Feathers Lodge crosses the Green Drive and skirts the upper end of Rhododendron Valley to enter the walled garden, which is now the car park. To the east is the water garden. This began as a small golf course but was subsequently developed with a sinuous pond, oriental pavilion (originally displayed at the Great Exhibition) and other oriental features, although it was never intended as a 'Japanese Garden'. Recently the garden has been expanded into the cherries, magnolias and rhododendrons around it, much to its benefit.

West of the walled garden the drive ends and the Shell Fountain of Sienna marble, made for W.W. Astor by Thomas Waldo Story, begins the north-south axis which continues along the double avenue of limes (heavily parasitized by mistletoe) through the forecourt, house, and terrace to the parterre below. The balustrade below the terrace, from the

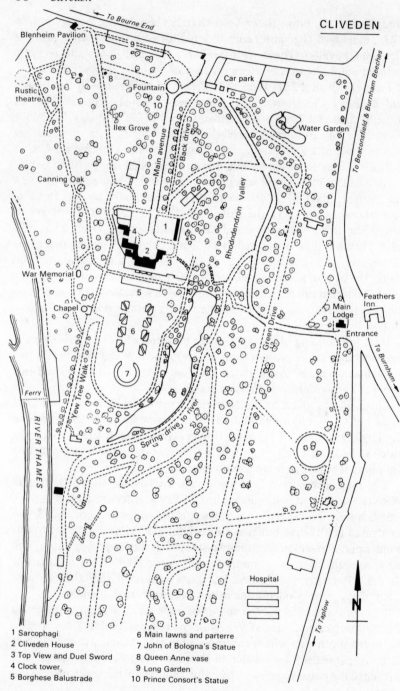

CLIVEDEN

To Bourne End

Blenheim Pavilion

To Beaconsfield & Burnham Beeches

Rustic theatre

Car park

Fountain

Water Garden

Ilex Grove

Main avenue

Back drive

Canning Oak

Rhododendron Valley

War Memorial

Green Drive

Chapel

Main Lodge

Feathers Inn

Entrance

To Burnham

Yew Tree Walk

Spring drive to river

Ferry

RIVER THAMES

Hospital

To Taplow

N

1 Sarcophagi
2 Cliveden House
3 Top View and Duel Sword
4 Clock tower
5 Borghese Balustrade
6 Main lawns and parterre
7 John of Bologna's Statue
8 Queen Anne vase
9 Long Garden
10 Prince Consort's Statue

Villa Borghese in Rome, and the bronze statue of Pluto and Prosperine which terminates the vista, were acquired by Viscount Astor.

East of this main axis, various paths descend through bluebell woods into Rhododendron Valley and eventually to the Thames. The picnic table, a disc from an enormous redwood trunk, still lies within the woods although the jacks which once elevated the table no longer operate!

West of the main axis there are many other features. Against the north boundary is the Long Garden, decorated with topiary. The long box-hedged herbaceous borders by Nancy Lindsay *c*.1900 disappeared many years ago but have now been replanted with variegated *Euonymus fortunei*. The wall still supports a fine collection of plants. Parallel to the Long Garden a grass ride extends from the Shell Fountain to a stone urn near the Blenheim Pavilion from which there are two walks along the hillside.

Between the upper walk and the lime avenue is the grove of *Quercus ilex* and, concealed within the woodland, an informal rose garden. Originally, and briefly, a rose garden *c*.1850, it became a bowling green then a tennis court before Geoffrey Jellicoe designed the present rose garden in 1959 for Lord Astor. The lower walk forks near the Canning Oak before descending to the Italian Garden (now a cemetery for 1914–18 casualties), the Leoni temple (now a chapel in which the 1st Viscount Astor is buried) and a yew-lined walk to the river.

Improvements by the National Trust are increasingly evident from year to year. In 1965 the parterre was re-established with box, *Santolina* and grass. In 1970 long herbaceous borders were planted in the forecourt. Designed by Graham Thomas, the east border is in strong colours, the west in pastels. In 1975 more extensive alterations began: extending and opening up the water garden, re-opening vistas through the woods, cutting back rhododendrons obscuring the smooth curve of the valley and, most recently, reducing in size the enormous yew hedges separating the avenue and forecourt. Cliveden has a wide range of plants but is especially notable for bulbs, both spring and autumn. These, too, have been planted in increasing numbers and variety, so visits early or late in the year are as rewarding as those made in summer.

Cokenach House, Barkway, Herts

13 acres; 1 gardener; clay soil. Open twice in May for NGS. 5 miles S of Royston and 3 miles E of A10.

Although now partly derelict, Cokenach is an old and interesting garden about which surprisingly little is known. The house was mentioned in the Domesday Book and a report of 1578 mentions fishing and interesting walks in the garden. The present house was begun in 1716 for the Chesters and it is probable that the moat which surrounded the older house was adapted to make the formal canals which still border the formal woodland. The south side of the moat was further modified between 1925 and 1946 to admit a tennis court and gardens.

The house now stands among lawns and tall trees on the north and west, with a remnant of the moat forming a shaded pool. To the south the main vista is along the central arm of the canal with formal walks along the banks and into the small wood. To the east a rose-lined walk leads around Victorian extensions to the orchard and walled garden, still productive. The vinery and other small greenhouses are grouped in a yard separate from the kitchen garden proper.

Compton Beauchamp, Wantage, Oxon

4 acres; 1½ gardeners; light soil over chalk, but with several springs. Open once in June for NGS. 7 miles W of Wantage, N of B4507 (Wantage–Swindon).

This twelfth-century moated manor-house was enlarged in 1583 and took on its present square plan by the addition of a classical front in 1710. The courtyard flanked by cottages and garages also dates from 1710 and with a short lime avenue, make an elegant approach to the north front.

The south garden, more or less rectangular in form, is terraced into a cross slope. It is enclosed by a high wall on the west side and formal banks merging into woodland on the east. Against the wall is a long herbaceous border, doubly impressive when it is first seen from the garden gate after a deeply shaded tunnel of evergreens. The path continues between yew hedges to a paeony garden and new rose garden tucked into a corner by the tennis court, which has shrub roses and geraniums along its long side.

On the east side a temple is set against dark yews bordering the 'monks' walk'. One can gain access to the hillside above either from the top of the garden or by steep steps near the ice-house by the moat.

The central axis of the garden rises in shallow terraces to wrought iron gates in the upper wall. On the lower level is a simple pattern of short and longer grass while, on the upper level, the more complicated outlines of a winter garden remain, with clipped greens, red-stemmed *Cornus*, winter-flowering shrubs and several fine *Acer griseum*. The central steps and borders were added in 1972 and were designed by Russel Smith of Waterers (as was the rose garden already mentioned).

Quite separate from the main garden, through the yard, is a new and very productive kitchen garden with greenhouses, frames, fruit cage and cut flowers as well as vegetables.

Cornwell Manor, Kingham, Oxon

---

15 acres formal garden plus extensive new tree planting; 2 gardeners; heavy loam over limestone. Open once in April and June/July for GS, NGS. 4 miles NW Chipping Norton off road to Kingham.

The gardens of Cornwell Manor are remarkable in many respects, not least in their recent origin. The house is Jacobean with eighteenth-century alterations but the garden, including the charming courtyard between the Jacobean and Georgian parts of the house, is entirely mid-twentieth-century. In 1936 the manor was bought by Mrs Gillson, who restored not only the house but the whole village. Clough Williams-Ellis was the architect, and his combination of elegance and warmth is felt throughout the garden.

The approach to the manor-house is over a stone bridge with a canalized stream flowing through the orchard on one side, then cascading down to a canal and formal pool in the valley on the other side.

From the house steps descend to the pool with steeper flights climbing the opposite bank to wrought iron gates on the road. Among the planting around the pool are some fine *Acer griseum*.

The stream is then released to wind between mossy rocks into two large lakes formed for ducks. The banks have been extensively planted with new trees from crab apples to large maples. This will soon require thinning but will eventually create a major feature.

West of the house is a large kitchen garden, only partly used. Sandwiched between its east wall and a massive double yew hedge along the back drive is a triangular garden with a swimming pool. The little garden full of lavender, roses and lilies has a fine semi-circular flight of steps up to the swimming pool and at the point of the garden, almost hidden by a weeping elm in the centre of another circle of steps, is a pavilion, again both elegant and charming.

East of the house is the newest part of the garden. The present owners, who came in 1958, have created a terraced chequer-board of a garden, firm in outline but softened by rounded hedges of box and lavender, beds and borders of roses and, as a feature on the axis leading to the little back courtyard, four weeping silver-leaved pears. Cornwell Manor is a delightful example of good architecture softened, not obliterated, by good planting and a refreshing contrast to the inadequate scale of so much new planting in large gardens.

Court Farm, Little Haseley, Oxon

5 acres; 1 gardener; alkaline clay except where altered. Open once in June for NGS. 8 miles SE Oxford. From M40 (Exit 7) turn SW onto A329, then first left to Great Haseley and continue along main road to Little Haseley.

Court Farm is an impressive example of what can be achieved in a short time by clear planning and bold action. In 1971 the remains of a small Victorian garden were bulldozed away and the first section of garden was completed in the following year, with two further sections of garden being developed in 1972/3 and 1973/4. Already the garden is well established and has a wide range of interesting trees, shrubs and other plants.

The owners wanted rhododendrons, roses, openness and informality. Their consultant, Kenneth Villiers, gave them this and much more.

Straight lines are avoided, except near the house where old barns and new stone walls unite house and garden. Even the stone wall around the tennis court and swimming pool is strongly curved and supports a heavily planted bank so that this part of the garden is invisible from elsewhere.

An open ride forms the spine of the garden. On one side are the rhododendrons, foreign features in this area but skilfully grouped on a polythene-lined bed of acid soil imported from Dorset. Roses and heathers skirt a small new 'woodland' of semi-mature trees concealing a vegetable garden and small orchid house. Finally earth-moving machinery has been used to create large mounds and a sunken bog garden. Here the process of adjusting water levels and planting is in its early stages but this promises to become an exciting feature.

On the other side of the main vista the steep bank concealing the swimming pool effectively balances, the view and from a raised walk along its summit new views of the garden can be obtained. An old apple tree, one of the few original plants, marks the end of the bank and masks the entrance to a circular lawn surrounded by limes and *Prunus laurocerasus* 'Zabelianiana'.

The silver garden, behind the house and sheltered between two barns, is quite separate. It houses the children's play equipment on a paved yard and central lawn, surrounded by raised borders of silver foliage. This combination of use and beauty is not to be missed.

Culham Court, Aston, Berks

About 10 acres; shallow soil over chalk. Open twice a year for GS, NGS. 1½ miles NE of Henley-on-Thames, on Berkshire side of river. Turn N off Remenham Hill near Five Horse Shoes Hotel, to Aston.

The garden at Culham Court merges imperceptibly into its surroundings, southwards into the beech-crowned scarp and north to the open meadows of the Thames so an estimate of its size is difficult. Much of the garden is fairly recent although *Sequoiadendron*, cedar, pines and tall yew hedges remain from an elaborate Victorian layout.

The south front of the house (1770) looks across the forecourt to a steep grassy bank scattered with large trees. Behind a Lawson's Cypress and large Judas Tree lies a remarkable rock garden, completely concealed, although it covers nearly half an acre. Designed in 1925 by Lady Barber (working first on a plasticine model) it begins as a winding grass dell with massive sandstone 'outcrops'. Steep winding steps lead up to rocky pinnacles and down to shady pools as the slope increases and although, like most rock gardens, it has had to be simplified, it remains very impressive. Many Japanese Maples and 'dwarf' conifers have reached large size, and small alpines have given way to more robust plants able to withstand the ravages of rabbits and peafowl.

Above the rock garden is a wild garden, now very overgrown, with drifts of narcissi and many different shrubs on the woodland fringe.

North of the house, terraces designed by Raymond Erith in 1957 descend between older yew hedges to the Thames. A swimming pool, also by Erith, nestles in a beautifully sculptured land form east of the terraces.

The $1\frac{1}{2}$ acre kitchen garden, down by the river, has much of interest although the old walls and low arched doorways (probably contemporary with an earlier house of 1706) do not make for efficient working. One unusual feature is a handsome *Cornus nuttallii*. Heeled in temporarily about 1950, it was forgotten until it flowered many years later, by which time it was too large to move.

Danes, Little Berkhamsted, Herts

---

2 acres; no gardener; acid sand and gravel over clay. Open once in June for NGS, RC or other charity. From B158 SW of Hertford, turn S into Robins Nest Lane.

Set among oak and birch woods, the garden at Danes has been much simplified in recent years, but remains peaceful and attractive. A terrace south and west of the house descends between old cut-leaved Japanese Maples to the lawn which winds around three sides of the house as an informal glade increasingly enclosed by banks of rhododendrons. An ancient yew, one of several nearby, half conceals the end of the house on which is a Banksian Rose. North of the house, twin borders form a vista into the enclosing woodland.

Danes Farm House ($\frac{1}{4}$ acre; no gardener) is also enclosed by woodland but is otherwise quite different in character. The steep south-west facing slope is terraced near the house and, apart from the central lawn, the whole garden is surrounded by interesting plants. As conditions vary in a few yards from the dry sunny bank on which aromatic plants flourish to spring-fed water garden and drier woodland margin, the range of plants is very impressive for a relatively small garden.

Ditchley Park, Enstone, Oxon (Ditchley Foundation)

180 acres; 2 gardeners plus estate team; alkaline clay-loam. Open for ten days late July to early August, 2–5. See HHCG. 12 miles NW of Oxford, 1½ miles W of A34 at Kiddington.

Built by Gibbs in 1722, Ditchley was long the seat of Lord Dillon. Third in size and date of the great Oxfordshire houses after Blenheim and Heythrop, it marks an important advance towards the refined Palladian taste of the age with interiors by William Kent and Henry Flitcroft. The park, with smooth lawns sloping between groups of beech to a lake, was discovered only recently to be the work of J.C. Loudon, incorporating such older features as the charming rotunda, possibly designed by Henry Holland *c.*1770. When the estate was sold in 1933, new formal gardens were designed by Geoffrey Jellicoe. Parterres overlook a sunken garden bordered by pleached limes and terminated by a semi-circular pool between intricate wings of yew. The north wing opens beneath a cedar to an eighteenth-century temple moved from the lakeside to terminate the long walk, carefully levelled among large limes and extending back along the house.

From its east end, near the house, there is just a glimpse of the rotunda. A mown walk through rough grass leads down to and around the lake, where groups of cherries and other small colourful trees planted in the 1930s add a gardenesque note.

Formal gardens were planned on a much larger scale, and the treatment of the broad vista south of the house shows how splendid this might have been on this high but relatively flat site. However, the war intervened and the estate was sold in 1949. Nine years later, after a further sale, the house and 180 acres of garden were endowed as an Anglo-American conference centre, continuing long-established links at Ditchley between the two nations. The rotunda and temple have been restored, the formal garden is well maintained and planned felling of over-mature trees may eventually re-establish the important landscape vistas between house and lake.

Donnington Castle House, Newbury, Berks

6 acres; 1 gardener; gravel soil over clay. Open once in June for NGS, and for local charities. 1 mile N of Newbury, turn W off B4494 (Newbury–Wantage) for Donnington.

Donnington Castle was held for the King during the Civil War until Colonel Dalbier, whose name survives in Dalbier's Mead, negotiated its surrender. The Castle House was enlarged in 1648, but the garden is much more recent, except for the tall limes south of the house. The 'Ladies Garden' behind a heavy studded door in the courtyard is also old in spirit although the planting, of grey foliage and copper/orange flowers against a low beech hedge, is modern. Festus Kelly created the garden, including the elaborate terrace walls around the croquet lawn east of the house, from 1920–40. The Parker-Bowles' reclaimed it after the war, adding many interesting shrubs and, following a brief but disastrous interlude when market gardening was the only activity, the present owners came in 1972, since which time many new and interesting trees have been added. The gates which provide such a fine entrance to the garden came from the old YMCA in Tottenham Court Road.

'Albertine' roses surround the croquet lawn below which is an area of rough grass with many bulbs and trees. The former kitchen garden is now planted with forest trees so vegetables are confined to the old walled yard north of the house, beside the tennis court and swimming pool.

Dalbier's Mead is the main part of the garden. This large bowl of grass surrounded by trees has a central vista of 'Nevada' roses down to a pool then up to a lime avenue. The bowl is emphasized by shrubs fringing the tree belt while many interesting trees have been planted in the lawn. An older lime avenue, outside the garden and now overgrown, still allows a peep up to the ruined castle.

Dower Cottage, Ardington, Oxon

½ acre; ½ gardener; loam over chalk. Open once in June or July for NGS. In Puddle Dock Lane, Ardington. S of A417 2½ miles E of Wantage.

It was only in 1973 that two cottages were combined and enlarged to make Dower Cottage but already the garden has a mature appearance. A new avenue of *Aesculus x carnea*, the Red Horse Chestnut, leads to the house.

On the north side the garden is compartmented and in shallow terraces. The central lawn is below two pools in small yew-enclosed gardens. The older pool garden is more formal with four rhododendrons in lead containers of peat and two of the astonishingly quick-growing *Abutilon vitifolium* framing the seat. Shrubs and small trees enclose two sides of the garden while the third side overlooks yet another pool in a sunken garden at the west end of the house.

To the south, the plan is more open. Large shrubs have been brought in to fill the border around an oval lawn and these are already so well established that care will be needed to retain the view which is part of the garden's charm.

Few gardens compress so much variety and intimacy into such a small space without losing the all-important sense of harmony. The fact that this has been achieved here in such a short time adds to the garden's interest, especially for other owners of new gardens.

Easneye, Ware, Herts

9 acres; 1 maintenance supervisor; gravel soil. Open once in May for RC. From E end of Stanstead Abbots turn N into Cappell Lane. From B1004 E of Ware turn S into Holly Cross Road.

The delightful gothic mansion of diaper brickwork, built by Alfred Waterhouse for the Buxton family, has housed All Nations Christian College since 1964. It is still partly clothed with ivies of green and gold, magnolias and other Victorian greenery but no elaborate gardens remain. However, vistas cut through the surrounding oak, chestnut and pine wood have been cleared and recovered from dereliction. The main vista extends south from the house, past the playing fields to the vegetable garden where half an acre of the original kitchen garden is being cultivated by students to supply most of the vegetables for the College.

Large beech and cedars around the house and occasional Red Oak and *Liquidambar* around the playing fields remain from the original garden and, north of the house, between new college buildings very much in sympathy with the old house, are courtyard plantings of heathers and junipers.

Edgcote, Chipping Warden, Oxon

6 acres plus 8-acre lake; 1 gardener; heavy loam over ironstone. Open by appointment only, Mons, May–Aug (see HHCG). 7 miles NE of Banbury on A361.

The garden at Edgcote is not listed as being of interest and certainly the main feature is the Palladian house with its mews grouped round a yard to one side. The lower yard with its cottages and kitchen garden completes a beautiful group of buildings all in the warm local stone.

However, the garden is certainly worth a visit. Near the house is a simple platform of grass with groups of rhododendrons separated from a dense shrubbery by a broad walk. An opening in the shrubbery near an enormous *Liriodendron* marks the entrance to a secluded flower garden which appears to have changed little for a century, although in fact it dates only from *c*.1920. A glasshouse and potting shed designed as a decorative pavilion leads to a sunken dahlia garden, a rose garden and formal pool, the whole surrounded by a horseshoe path bordered with iris and leading to a glade of scattered shrubs and small trees.

Across the grass terrace, the ground falls and there is much new planting of trees and rhododendrons around the tennis court. A gate at the lower end of the garden leads to a delightful watermill (now disused), a bright cottage garden and back, along the road, to the house and its church.

Elcot Park Hotel, Newbury, Berks

16 acres; 2½ gardeners; acid gravel soil. Open once in late April and late May for NGS. 5 miles W of Newbury on N side of A4.

Designed by Sir William Paxton in 1848, Elcot Park was a fine Victorian country house, well sited on a south slope with distant views. The garden was carefully planned with respect to orientation and variety of effect. In 1945, after long neglect, it became an hotel and, from 1966, efforts have been made to improve the garden. Ten years of restoration have resulted in a generally well-maintained appearance spoiled only by the poorly sited swimming pool and car park.

The entrance from the west is between banks planted thickly with daffodils. To the south the principal view is framed by hedges, while a terraced grass walk leads from the south front, past the west lawn (once a parterre of flower beds) to a dark grove of cedars and Wellingtonias. To the east a larger horseshoe walk leads among large rhododendrons and bamboos with a fringe of oaks.

North of the house the kitchen garden was once a major feature with a shrub-lined walk to its main entrance. Against its south wall something of the Victorian character remains with tile-edged gravel paths through the shrubbery now dominated by a large multi-trunked *Cercidiphyllum*. The kitchen garden itself has now been grassed over but glasshouses, cross paths, the central dipping pond and wall-trained fruit trees are still evident.

34 Elm Avenue, Oxhey, Watford, Herts

⅛ acre; no gardener; clay soil much modified. Open by appointment for NGS. SE edge of Watford off A4008.

Not many gardens can boast a soil of John Innes quality but 34 Elm Avenue has just this. The garden was begun in 1972 by roughly digging the heavy clay soil then thick layers of peat, leaf-mould and sand were incorporated with a rotary cultivator. As a result the soil level is raised, giving good drainage, and there are more sandy and more peaty spots in the garden just right for certain plants.

Like other gardens open by appointment, it is small, crammed with plants and very interesting. It is also neatly kept and beautifully labelled and catalogued, befitting the garden of a retired librarian. The plan is simple: a curving border along the east side frames a lawn which narrows to a winding path through the dense planting in the' farther half of the garden, returning in a loop to the lawn alongside the greenhouse. York stepping stones in the borders facilitate access to plants.

There are nearly 2,000 species in total, varying in stature from eventually large trees such as *Ginkgo*, *Liquidambar* and *Parrotia* to small bulbs and alpines. All are well labelled. *Ericaceae* are numerically most important, including 30 rhododendrons ranging from the tiny *R.radicans* upwards. The family *Liliaceae* is also well represented by *Colchicum*, fritillaries, *Trillum* and about 200 lilies. Although plants appear and disappear almost daily there is seldom a month without some hardy cyclamen in flower.

Englefield House, Theale, Berks

12-acre garden (excluding commercial walled garden) in large estate; 2 gardeners; clay soil. Open once in May for NGS. 4 miles W of Reading. From roundabout on A4 W of Theale, turn N towards Pangbourne. Entrance gates ½ mile on left.

Englefield House occupies the eastern tip of the long curved ridge separating the rivers Pang and Kennet. Although not high at this point, it offers extensive views over the deer park, lakes, and Kennet valley.

The garden is on the south-east and south-west sides of the tall Elizabethan house. The lower garden is formal and although simplified, is very much in scale with the house. In the west corner of the main terrace is a new (1975) border of grey-leaved and tender plants sheltered below the old part of the house. Its line continues below stone balustrades with a delightful colour-graded border of yellow fading to white by a central pool and finally to the soft pink of shrub roses before merging with a bank of enormous Japanese Maples. Above this bank is an informal garden on the natural undulations of two shallow ridges. The larger ridge to the south west is scattered with redwoods, beech and oak, beneath which walks wind through huge mounds of rhododendrons. A perimeter path continues below the reservoir to return down the second ridge with smaller scale plantings of maples, *Viburnum*, *Magnolia*, etc. in clearings among the larger trees, and hence into the open above the house.

The little valley between is emphasized by the trees and a tumbling stream. Informal garden meets formal on open terraces of grass, partly embanked, partly walled. Here, as elsewhere in the garden, the rougher grass is thickly planted with bulbs.

A two-acre walled garden away from the house is separately staffed and run commercially. It is open during normal business hours and is worth visiting to see well-trained fruit which remains interspersed with commercial glasshouses.

Epwell Mill, Banbury, Oxon

2 acres; part-time help with lawn and hedges; heavy loam. Open once in April, May and June/July for NGS. 7 miles W of Banbury, N of B4035 (Banbury–Shipston-on-Stour) between Shutford and Epwell.

At first impression this is a typical cottage garden. The large vegetable patch is only half concealed by a hedge at the entrance and the approach between the long, low cottage and the barn is up a cobbled slope covered with thyme. Millstone steps, tubs of 'geraniums' and hydrangeas and borders of old herbaceous perennials around the lawn under apple trees all add to the effect.

After such an introduction, the new south garden, designed by Geoffrey Smith of Warwick to replace a tennis court in 1962, comes as a considerable surprise yet it fits entirely appropriately into the garden. The steep cross slope is terraced with pools, paving, steps, hornbeam hedges and shrubs interlocking in three giant steps. The lowest flight of steps continues along a path of herringbone brick to yew- and box-hedged borders. Formerly a rose garden, these borders have been re-planted with yellow and purple foliage: the greys of lavender and catmint remain from the rose garden. An edging continues, as a thin dividing arc between the lawn and a gentle mound of rougher grass planted with bulbs, to a circular pool. A stepping-stone path among azaleas and small trees opens above the terraces and the mill stream.

There are more interesting plants against the south and west walls of the house but the major feature is the water garden. From a simple pond above the vegetable garden, a winding stream flows through large groups of *Primula, Meconopsis,* ferns and *Iris.* Water also flows by pipe to two large lily tanks (the higher tank formerly a very cold swimming pool!) and back over shallow falls to meet the stream at the sluice, below which the water has hollowed a large natural basin in the rock.

Fanhams Hall, Ware, Herts (Building Societies' Staff College)

27 acres; 3—5 gardeners; clay soil. Open four days a year for NGS etc. 1 mile NE of Ware. From A10 in Ware turn off by Bell Hotel up New Road and Musley Hill Road. Right at end of road.

Fanhams Hall garden provides an appropriate late-Victorian setting for the large house, built in 1901 on the site of a smaller Queen Anne house. There are many unusual plants throughout the garden and styles range from the formal terraced rose garden to a fine Japanese garden.

Around the house are small rectilinear gardens: a scented garden near the car park, a grey garden on a dry south-west facing terrace and a knot garden leading down to 'Queen Anne's Garden' with rose arches and borders of pastel flowers. The main lawn, terminated by full-moon arches, looks over Queen Anne's Garden to walks of pleached lime, some very old, others planted in 1905. The limes border a croquet lawn with a huge *Arbutus unedo* at one end. The rose garden below the house has sheltered borders of unusual shrubs and a border of variegated shrubs on the outer side. Here are gathered variegated forms of many familiar shrubs and even the H.T. rose 'Curiosity'.

A huge lotus bowl in the rose-garden pool provides a cue for the Japanese garden beyond. A wisteria-clad pergola leads to the three-acre garden with its 'fox' lake, tea-house, bridges, lanterns, dry 'waterfalls', maples and pines. Many features were brought from Japan and in its heyday Japanese gardeners were imported each summer.

Other small ponds provide settings for the Swiss chalet and Austrian pavilion from the 1901 exhibition while earth from the Swiss lake was used to create a 'Mount Fuji'. The once verdant mountain, with winding paths to the summit, has suffered from erosion but it still presents a remarkable spectacle.

Large borders have been planted recently in the field west of the rose garden so the variety of effects within the garden continues to increase.

Faringdon House, Faringdon, Oxon

10 acres plus park and lake; 1 gardener; heavy calcareous loam. Open one weekend in April for GS, NGS. In Faringdon (15 miles SW Oxford) next to church on road to Witney.

Faringdon House was built by John Wood of Bath in 1760 on the site of a much larger Tudor house destroyed by Cromwell.

From the entrance lodge the drive runs north through a shaded carpet of bulbs, sweeps round in front of the house and returns southwards through a grove of old limes and elms marking an earlier entrance. The yews which shade the drive enclose, on their other side, an open, gently-terraced lawn leading up from the house to the church. A long walk lined with lilacs and *Staphylea holocatpa* borders the churchyard to complete a square, the lines of which extend to encompass distant views.

Statues and urns are important features throughout the garden. A figure of 'Greece' stands appropriately in the grove while 'Egypt' surveys the Witney road from a former gun emplacement. Both statues came from the Crystal Palace.

West of the drive is the kitchen garden, over two acres of south-west slope margined on the upper side by massive Tudor walls and lined with seasonal herbaceous borders including a paeony garden. Below the kitchen garden is the orangery, rescued from a wilderness about 1960. The natural landform slopes away from the orangery but a large embankment of rubble reverses the slope, forming an amphitheatre surrounded by dark foliage. The orangery now stands above a pool, facing a grand stairway rising to the sky. Urns around the pool came from Versailles.

Paths from the orangery and kitchen garden unite above a small valley by a large urn from the Crystal Palace, where once an elaborate water garden extended to the bridge. The lake was created in 1800 by enlarging an older fish pond and the summerhouse was built soon after as an eye-catcher from the house. Behind the summerhouse steep steps lead down through a fernery which is still being planted.

The valley rim has a curving path heavily enclosed by flowering cherries and shrubs. This dense growth will eventually be removed to reveal an avenue of Monkey Puzzle, at present only a few feet high.

Filkins Mill, Filkins, Oxon

1 acre; no gardener; heavy loam over gravel. Open twice in May/June for GS, NGS. 3½ miles N of Lechlade (Glos) between Filkins and Langford.

When Filkins Mill was restored in 1967–9 the mill workings were removed but two streams remain as major features. A low wall encloses an inner garden. Roses, jasmine, a nectarine and *Cytisus battandieri* benefit from sheltering walls while walnut and a young Judas tree increase the enclosure.

South of the mill stream, now fed by a pipe beneath the house, the garden is open and undulating. The walls of the stream flatten into the rocky banks of a colourful waterside garden. In spring there are Rock Roses and other rock plants near the house. Later, many herbaceous plants benefit from the open situation and adequate moisture. *Phlox, Ligularia* and montbretia are particularly colourful.

The garden is high and increasingly exposed as elm hedgerows die off. In January 1976 a group of six large elms blew down creating enormous damage but the loss was not entirely harmful. Freed of dense shade and dense roots, the exposed bank is being planted with more interesting material and there is now a better view of the shrubbery by the gate. Begun with a gift of hypericums in 1973, this now includes many other good shrubs. In addition to its own attractiveness, the definite end which it provides to the southern half of the garden emphasizes the depth and perspective of the west part across the stream.

North of the house is the vegetable garden. In the north-west corner, concealing the flood channel, are young fruit trees, roses, a small island border of herbaceous plants and a flourishing young *Davidia*. Other flowering trees are being added as elms die off and the garden continues to grow in interest year by year.

Fishers, Shepherd's Green, Oxon

3 acres; part-time gardener; shallow clay over chalk. Open once in June or July for NGS (see also *White Cottage* which is adjacent). 4 miles W of Henley-on-Thames, via road to Rotherfield Greys, bear right after village green.

This is essentially a spring garden as much has been grassed down leaving large fruit trees underplanted with narcissi. Near the house, however, yew hedges surround a formal rose garden with thick clumps of *Lilium regale*, and an opening in the hedge leads to herbaceous borders. For these the garden is open in summer. The vegetable garden, although recently halved, remains productive and interesting.

Beyond the lawn is a neighbour's tiny garden, which is also opened. Roses, clematis, pinks and herbaceous plants jostle together in a colourful border around the small lawn.

Folly Farm, Sulhamstead, Berks

7 acres; 2½ gardeners; gravel soil. Open once in May for GS. 8 miles SW of Reading. From A4 turn S 2 miles W of Theale, then ¾ mile.

Folly Farm is unmistakably a Lutyens and Gertrude Jekyll design and the house itself is interesting in that the lower and apparently older part, nestling beneath a deep tiled roof, is actually an addition (in 1913) to the more classical house of 1906.

The main gardens are to the south, where the natural slope is terraced to form a series of distinct compartments. In the long pool garden, the end of the pool is lost in shade beneath a wisteria-hung balustrade. The purple garden is spacious and colourful with wide bor-

ders, smooth lawns and brick paths around the massive central slab of
Purbeck marble. In the sunken garden planting is confined to beds of
low roses lest the intricate interwoven pattern of steps, paths and pool
be obscured.

Away from the house, limes, fruit trees and flowering trees freely
underplanted with bulbs line the various walks extending towards the
kitchen garden. With tile-coped walls and arched gates, the kitchen
garden itself is handsome but Lutyens banished the glasshouses to the
outside of the wall where they form a picturesque but inconvenient
group. The kitchen garden, reduced by the later inclusion of a tennis
court, is run semi-commercially.

Beyond the enclosed gardens formal gives way to informal open
grass studded with large trees. A deep rhododendron border added by
the present owners creates a long informal vista and conceals a steep-
sided water garden.

Although the days when there were ten gardeners are long past, the
garden remains largely intact. Many characteristic plants remain, from
pleached limes to hostas, and even the two quince placed above the long
pool by Gertrude Jekyll have healthy young replacements. Severe
pruning of misshapen *Quercus ilex* along the roadside in the wake of elm
felling, and the cutting back of the yew hedge around the sunken
garden, temporarily exposing the swimming pool, appear drastic, but
indicate the continued wellbeing of this important garden.

Foxgrove, Enborne, Berks

1 acre; part-time help with digging & mowing; neutral clay loam. Open
once in April for NGS. 2½ miles SW of Newbury. From A343 (Newbury–
Andover) turn W at 'The Gun', 1½ miles from town centre.

The original flower garden at Foxgrove, enclosed by a small orchard on
the south, vegetables on the east, a large drive on the north and the
road on the west, consisted of a herbaceous border and rock garden
around a small lawn. When the garden was revived in 1968 a central
swathe of the border was grassed down, reducing the weeding required
and simultaneously opening views into the triangular orchard. Since
then the fruit trees have been interspersed with rhododendrons and
roses. Bulbs flourish in the grass and clematis scramble into the trees.

The rock garden is gradually being replanted and alpines are already established in a low dry wall along part of the drive. A narrow strip between the house and road, shaded by *Eucalyptus* and a thriving *Prunus incisa*, is devoted to woodland plants while, in sharp contrast, the dry wall and entrance a few feet away support collections of *Sempervivum* and *Iris unguicularis*.

The result is a flourishing family garden, maintained by an enthusiast whose widening interests include snowdrops, *Helleborus*, *Primula* and *Eucalyptus*, all well represented in the garden.

Frogmore Gardens, Windsor Castle, Berks

30 acres; 4 gardeners; clay soil over chalk. Open on first Wed and Thur in May, 11–7 for NGS, by gracious permission of HM the Queen. Entrance through Long Walk Gate in Windsor. See also *Windsor Great Park* for *Savill Garden* and *Valley Gardens*.

Unlike Savill and Valley Gardens to the south, Frogmore is situated on the flat clay soil of former marshland below the castle. The garden was designed in 1793 by Major William Price, Vice-Chamberlain to Queen Charlotte. By digging out a serpentine lake and using the spoil to form large mounds, Price created a garden of great variety and charm, decorated with exotic and rustic summerhouses in the best traditions of Georgian landscape gardening.

Unfortunately it was neglected throughout the nineteenth century and not until Queen Mary took an interest in the garden was it rescued. Under her guidance thickets were cleared and many trees, shrubs and bulbs were planted from 1918 to 1939. After the war further improvements were made, despite the ravages of alternate floods and drought in 1946/7, so that the garden now contains a wide variety of shrubs bordering the winding walks.

The large mausoleum in which Queen Victoria and the Prince Consort are buried dominates the entrance to the garden. This and the smaller mausoleum of Queen Victoria's mother, the Duchess of Kent, are also open on both days.

The Garden House, Cottered, Herts

6 acres; 1 gardener; sandy soil. Open once in June for RC, and once for Church fund. 3 miles W of A10 between Buntingford (3 miles) and Baldock (6 miles) or Stevenage (7 miles).

Although there were several Japanese gardens constructed in England early in this century most have disappeared or been anglicized beyond recognition. The garden at Cottered no longer has 14 gardeners pinching the buds of pines and spruce to maintain the scale of the garden, but it remains one of the best and most sympathetically kept Japanese gardens in the country.

Herbert Goode's visit to Japan in 1905 stimulated him to acquire several lanterns and other works of art. In the same year he began to shape a miniature landscape of mountains and lakes from a flat pasture. More plants and buildings were brought from Japan and from 1923–26 Seyemon Kusumoto completed the design, with minor additions and alterations until Mr Goode died in 1937. The garden was restored in 1964 and The Garden House built in 1966.

The garden is surrounded by a fence of beautiful workmanship. From the Gateway of the Feudal Lord paths of carefully composed stones penetrate the garden between carpets of dwarf bamboo, from which rise taller bamboos, maples, pines and spruce. Each hill, each turn in the path has its own significance with lanterns and tori to mark important points. The tea-house, thatched resting-house and an exquisite two-storied pavilion called 'Pure Heart' provide attractive garden features and points from which the best composed views of the garden can be contemplated. The last-mentioned building was enlarged in 1964 as a guest-house.

Central to the garden is the sinuous 'Fox Lake' crossed and recrossed by red-painted bridges. One of the most delightful crossings is by stepping stones beneath a cantilevered canopy of wisteria. The lake is filled by a Linen waterfall, falling unbroken from a shaded mountain pool. The pine-clad hill from which it emerges is the highest of the several hills which surround the garden, creating a garden quite apart from the world outside.

Giles Farm, Stoke Row, Oxon

4 acres; part-time gardener; medium loam over chalk. Open once in June for GS/NGS. 7 miles N of Reading. Stoke Row is signposted from A4009 (Reading–Nettlebed) and Giles Farm is at W end of village.

Yew hedges and flint walls to the south and the terracing of a gentle slope to the north divide the garden at Giles Farm into a series of varied compartments grouped with easy informality around the seventeenth-century farmhouse.

Statuesque Scots Pines dominate the entrance court from which one can enter the rose garden (the easiest route for wheelchairs). However, a dark group of hawthorn and yews provides a more inviting approach, revealing a glimpse of the main lawn as one draws near. The lawn is surrounded by borders of soft colours in contrast to the brighter colours of the adjacent rose garden. The orchard extends the full length of the south boundary and is an attractive feature with many climbing and shrub roses among the trees.

Behind the house is a herb garden, overflowing with aromatic plants and surrounded by climbers. The remainder of this north garden is more open. The gentle slope has been terraced to admit paths along the top and bottom beside which borders extend to a tall shrub border concealing the garage. The lower border is filled with mounds of sun-loving plants, while the upper border, with more shade, has herbaceous perennials beneath old pear trees swathed in clematis and roses. As a focal point in the lawn, an aged tree almost immersed in green and gold ivy has a young climbing rose forming a second layer of more fleeting beauty.

Although most visitors will come on a June afternoon, it is worth noting the many plants which have been included in the garden for winter interest or for fragrance at dusk and in early morning, times when much of the work is done in this delightful garden.

Great Rollright Manor, Chipping Norton, Oxon

4 acres; 1 gardener; alkaline clay-loam. Open once in July for NGS. From A34 midway between Oxford and Stratford, turn off N at signpost to Great Rollright, then 1 mile.

The sweep of drive around three sides of the manor-house cuts into the hill, creating curved banks on which stand large sycamores. The trees, land form and house form a beautiful composition. There are flowering cherries and shrub roses near the entrance and roses occur in greater numbers in a border south of the walled kitchen garden. On the east lawn laburnums associate well with the grove of *Quercus ilex*.

The south terrace looks over the lawn and paddock to a small lake embanked above the steep slope. The lake and garden are connected by a narrow woodland walk in which scattered shrubs and groups of hostas, alchemilla, hellebores etc. provide enclosure and interest. This walk reveals first the source of the lake, a spring beneath another large sycamore. In the deep shade, the steep-sided dell has been made into a shrub garden, opening beyond to the grassy banks of the lake with duck and distant views for further interest.

Greys Court, Henley-on-Thames, Oxon (The National Trust)

5 acres; 1 gardener; thin chalk soil. Open April–Sept, Mon–Sat, 2.15–6. (House: Mon, Wed, Fri only.) See HHCG. 3 miles NW of Henley on road to Peppard.

After a long history, during which it has been altered to a greater or lesser extent by almost every generation of its owners, Greys Court remains in character a family home. The admiration of Sissinghurst by its most recent owners, Sir Felix and Lady Brunner, is revealed in many garden features, the white garden, rose garden and nut walk for example. Greys Court is an appropriate site for such emulation with its lofty tower, and many walls. Like the house, however, the garden retains a quiet, family atmosphere.

The sixteenth-century house, within the courtyard of de Grey's mediaeval house, was much altered in 1750. Most other buildings are Tudor although the well within the wheelhouse dates from the original dwelling, of which the Great Tower and three of the four smaller towers remain (two incorporated in later buildings). The Great Tower provides an excellent vantage point from which to gain an overview of the garden.

The base of the tower is mounded with aromatic plants suited to the south-west aspect overshadowed by tall Scots Pines. From the fore-court between house and tower, the ground rises northwards to an area of scattered trees and shrubs including *Arbutus unedo* and *A.andrachne*. The bridge over the ha-ha, with its full-moon gate, was made from a Chinese pattern in Oxford in 1964. West of the house is an enormous larch, one of three notable trees in the garden. The other two, a Weeping Ash and a Tulip Tree near the south-east ha-ha, appear to have altered little since their depiction in an engraving dated 1823.

East of the tower is a series of irregular walled gardens. The white garden with its central pool, the semi-circular garden of huge wisterias and the rose garden are interconnected. The rose garden has a yellow and a pink border and a flourishing Banksian Rose among other features. The wisterias, planted about 1850, now have enormous twisting trunks.

The kitchen garden was grassed down in 1976/7 but the arch of *Robinia hispida* in the rose garden, brought originally from Friar Park at Henley, has been copied to permit its extension through the kitchen garden. Outside the east wall is a nut walk and polyanthus border, leading to the wild garden with its carpet of daffodils. South of the kitchen garden is another small walled garden, in fact a roofless tithe barn. It was planted with cherries in 1951 as a spring garden, and is shaded by the huge *Liriodendron*. A sun-baked paved corner west of the rose garden leads back to the Carlisle Collection of miniature rooms, the house itself and the donkey-wheel, the largest surviving example of its type. It was used until 1914. A horse-wheel from Shabden has been re-erected to the west of the wheelhouse.

The house, other buildings and 280 acres of land were given to the National Trust in 1969 by Sir Felix Brunner.

Haddenham Gardens, Bucks

Several gardens varying in size and character but all developed and maintained by their owners. Soil heavy alkaline clay changing to greensand near the railway. Open once in June for NGS; plants, produce and cakes sold. 1½ miles S of A418 between Thame (3 miles) and Aylesbury (6 miles), at Church End.

16 Church End (⅔ acre): This is a small, sheltered garden of irregular shape, surrounded by high walls. A low wall within the garden also separates the pleasure garden from the kitchen garden in which different unusual vegetables are tried each year. The division is not complete however, as narrow borders around the vegetable garden are filled with iris, early bulbs and other plants benefitting from this alkaline, heavy but well-drained soil.

The south-east quarter of the garden is planted with sufficient depth to admit narrow winding paths, one of which leads to a small rocky sunken garden. Narrower borders along the other walls enclose a lawn which, by virtue of the irregular shape of the garden as a whole, curves in an informal vista to the end of the garden with its summerhouse, greenhouse and small pool.

Croft Thatch, 1 The Croft (¼ acre): Hollyhocks towering over the low wall by this 350-year-old thatched cottage form an appropriate introduction to a truly 'cottage garden'. Behind the cottage, the tapering plot is divided into four very unequal parts by a cross path, each part being used to grow plants suited to the various aspects offered with no rigid segregation of flowers, fruits and vegetables.

Near the cottage a large weeping willow overhangs the well, creating a shady corner in which spring bulbs, foxgloves and alpine strawberries flourish. The shade is emphasized by edgings of raspberry and of espalier fruit underplanted with lilies. A small sunny corner by the conservatory has a raised bed of iris and alstroemeria with an herbaceous border along the remaining east boundary. The fourth part, in contrast, is open lawn, bordered by a little stream in which mimulus flourishes.

To continue the mixture, currant bushes, rugosa roses and herbs form a group in the lawn, with a hedge of asparagus at the end. Vegetables are grown in any available spaces in the borders while alpine strawberries, hollyhocks and foxgloves are allowed to seed wherever there is room, creating a charmingly casual atmosphere.

Diggs Field, 19 Station Road (1 acre): Diggs Field is a large garden to retire to but it is being planned for ease of maintenance in future years. The house, of attractive modern design, is in one corner of the slightly undulating square plot. The main feature of the garden is a curving border along most of the east side, with an outlying island of low thymes in scale with the small deck extending from the house. Annuals are used less and less as shrubs fill their allotted space and emphasis is placed on plants for year-round attractiveness of foliage and form. To encourage wildlife, the garden is not over-tidied: nettles attract butter-flies, cotoneasters and other fruiting plants attract birds, and climbing plants on sloping frames provide moist conditions for frogs.

Along the west side of the garden beds of heathers, shrub roses and more small trees partially conceal the boundary and the vegetable garden.

A feature of particular interest is the large central island of long grass. Mown only three or four times a year, ostensibly to save work, this long grass and the long border define a sweeping curve of shorter grass which accentuates the subtle ground form. This island then is an im-portant element of this attractive garden, especially when yellow with buttercups or bulbs.

Grenville Manor, Aston Road (¾ acre): Although the house is old and attractive, it sits almost in the middle of a flat square plot of heavy clay, a most unpromising prospect. From 1971, however, the garden began to take shape. Two rectangular beds in the lawn (over manhole covers) each have a pair of Irish yew columns which, with a pair halfway along the flower-lined path and a central sundial, form an axis across the garden. A bed of fine bearded iris backed by purple-leaved cotinus and *Rosa rubrifolia* draws the eye across the garden to a low mixed border concealing a small vegetable garden.

In contrast to the openness of most of the garden, a weeping willow behind the house and studio creates a cool shady corner in which hostas and hellebores are establishing.

Hill View, 37 Churchway (½ acre): How often is the mystery of an over-grown garden lost when new owners tidy it out of existence? Hill View offers a lesson in selective reclamation in which enclosure and interest have been preserved by keeping some of the overgrowth either per-manently or until it can be replaced by better plants. In 1971 the tangle of elder, plum suckers and nettles had been cleared sufficiently to begin planting and already the winding path from the house to an old apple tree forms an established garden complete in itself although it occupies only a quarter of the plot.

Two small borders complete the circle around the apple and partly conceal the vegetables. The walk continues through a small orchard parallel to the vegetable plot and terminates in a little fern garden tucked away in the corner. A change of surface from grass to sawn logs emphasizes the separation of this little dell. The other corner of the garden is still being reclaimed and several new shrubs indicate steady progress.

In complete contrast to the main garden, the minute front garden of Hill View is paved, with many low and trailing plants growing in the crevices.

Swanbourne, 21 Church End ($\frac{1}{2}$ acre): This long thin garden is divided into three approximately equal parts, occupied by the house and drive, a lawn flanked by borders and the kitchen garden.

The house itself is attractive with a narrow sun-baked border at its foot. Across the drive a wider border is heavily shaded by willow and apple trees, filled with *Viburnum plicatum* 'Lanarth' and carpeted with ferns, hostas and bulbs to create a cool green retreat. A conservatory, small greenhouse and herb border are behind the house, convenient to the kitchen.

The lawn, on a higher level than the drive, is flanked by stone paths so plants in the twin borders can spill freely onto and into the paths. One border is mainly of blue and white, the other red and yellow. At either end of the lawn are smaller beds filled with tiny pinks, thymes, dwarf bulbs and other low plants, many raised from seed and many labelled.

The kitchen garden is a model of neatness, befitting a garden owned by a skilled surgeon and an equally skilled embroiderer. Fruit trees of all kinds are trained on the walls (which run the full length of the garden and are of the local white clay), vegetables occupy the centre while the fruit cage, with closely spaced cordons of gooseberry and currants, is a joy to behold.

The Ham, Wantage, Oxon

5 acres; 1 gardener; shallow clay over chalk. Open once in April for NGS. On W edge of Wantage. Entrance lodge opposite Ham Road on road to Swindon.

Although this is a large, flat garden, it is dissected by the Letcombe Brook. Arising at the foot of the Downs, it divides here into three streams then re-unites, so there are two islands within the garden, and the sound of water is never far away.

The main garden feature is the long island east of the entrance. Once a nuttery and for many years a rubbish dump, it has been cleared and replanted since 1963. One unusual problem here is that decaying tree roots create natural water pipes which gradually enlarge, causing subsidence. The irregular holes are concealed by ground-cover planting almost as quickly as they form, and large-scale planting of herbaceous plants (*Acquilegia, Polygonum, Geranium,* etc.) beneath the remaining beech and birch have transformed the former dump into a charming wild garden. Bulbs, especially *Narcissus,* also flourish.

Across the drive is the orchard, also thickly planted with bulbs.

South of the house, the garden is much more open. The second, larger island is mown infrequently, but closely mown paths lead to a small rose garden. Across the stream is a croquet lawn and long herbaceous border. The wall backing this border was rebuilt in 1976 following severe storm damage. It conceals the kitchen garden, half of which is still used.

The garden is open in the spring for its many bulbs but the borders, new tree planting, wild garden and new 'meadow-garden' extend the season of interest.

Hambleden Manor House, Hambleden, Bucks

5 acres; 3 gardeners; clay with flints over chalk. Open once in April and June for NGS. 4 miles NE of Henley-on-Thames, 1 mile N of A4155 (Henley–Marlow) from Mill End.

The Manor House stands above the village on a steep west-facing slope. From the gate, the drive encircles a huge copper beech below the house. North of the drive a path along an old shrub border enters the partly walled kitchen garden which still produces quantities of vegetables, flowers and plants for the house. To the south is another walled garden, but of a very different kind. In 1970 an informal swimming pool and elegant summerhouse were made in the high-walled enclosure and the garden was planted with lavender, grey-leaved plants and other subjects thriving in this hot and sheltered position.

The swimming pool garden is equally attractive from above: a terrace along the south front of the house looks over the lawn to a border of shrub roses, from the lower end of which one overlooks the pool garden. The house itself supports a large Banksian rose and *Vitis coignetiae*. The conservatory, built in 1960, has its own interesting collection of climbers and tender plants growing in borders around the wall.

From this east end of the terrace a path climbs steeply across the sloping hillside and around the house among large limes and sycamores. Above the house, flowering cherries and shrub roses are planted in the grass and everywhere there are drifts of bulbs: snowdrops, daffodils and, on the lower slopes especially, *Cyclamen repandum* and *Chederifolium*. The winding path returns above the kitchen garden to a particularly large lime and a trio of *Liquidambar styraciflua* nearer the drive.

Hartwell House, Aylesbury, Bucks (House of Citizenship)

4 acres; 1 gardener; clay soil. Open Wed p.m., May–mid-July (see HHCG).
2 miles SW of Aylesbury on N side of A418 (Aylesbury–Thame).

The seat of the Lee family for nearly four centuries to 1936, Hartwell House has an interesting history, an interest which spills over into the gardens.

The seventeenth-century formal gardens, with arcades of yew, pools, statues and garden buildings are no more. Sir William Lee, 4th baronet, married Lady Elizabeth Harcourt, only daughter of Simon Earl Harcourt of Nuneham (which see), and not surprisingly, Lancelot Brown was called in to informalize the surroundings of Sir William's newly enlarged house. William Mason also visited Hartwell frequently after the marriage, and the pleasure garden may well have been influenced by his ideas.

The house was later leased to the Comte de Provence, exiled heir to the French throne, who derived much pleasure from the gardens. It was at Hartwell in 1814 that he was crowned Louis XVIII and on his return to France he made an 'English garden' at the Tuileries to remind him of his former home.

Multiple tenancy now prevents the exploration of the whole park but the chapel and bridge are near the north front of the house and the pleasure garden remains within the ha-ha on the south front.

Stone paths wind through old yews on the east side of the garden to return through the beech grove concealing the kitchen garden and stables on the west. Among the beech, a statue of George II on horseback is another reminder of royal visitors. The beech and yews frame the lawn and a circular lily pool surrounded by recently replanned borders. West of the pool is a *Liriodendron tulipifera*, planted in 1881. To the south is an old *Cryptomeria japonica* 'Elegans' which has fallen apart to form an undulating mound some 50 feet across. East of the pool two of the yews remaining from the old formal garden are now clipped to represent the crown and mitre of Louis XVIII.

Haseley Court and Coach House, Little Haseley, Oxford

10 acres; 3 gardeners; alkaline clay. Open once in June for NGS. 8 miles SE Oxford. From M40 (Exit 7) turn SW onto A329 then first left to Great Haseley and continue along main road to Little Haseley.

The garden of Haseley Court, an ideal setting for its Queen Anne house, appears to have changed little with the centuries. However, apart from the famous topiary planted about 1850, the whole garden was created *after* 1955, from the gravelled forecourt with its raised dais to the intricate quartered pattern of the walled garden. During long neglect, the topiary was saved by an old man in the village who, unasked and unaided, kept the figures carefully trimmed while lawns and borders degenerated into hayfields and thickets.

Now the topiary forms a sunken parterre, an intricate pattern of santolina and lavender contrasting with dark clipped box. The 'knight' in the south-east corner of the parterre was improvised from two box bushes in 1973 following the demise of his predecessor but already fits remarkably well into the scheme. Yews surround three sides of the parterre and on the fourth side steps lead up through the white borders to the main terrace.

East of the house, ancient foundations were too numerous to permit normal gardening so clipped yews with skirts of ivy are raised on individual mounds of topsoil. From this corner a path leads past compartmented herbaceous borders on the left with views through the bulb-strewn woodland on the right to the moat, a shaded panel of water which once formed part of a larger system of ponds.

A dense nutwood underplanted with *Helleborus orientalis* fills the corner between moat and house, opening into a little clearing north of the moat. Swirls of box narrow the opening and edge a long narrow alley outside which occasional glimpses of hornbeam hedge serve as astonishing reminders of the time when this was an open windswept field. From the alley another opening leads to the walled garden.

The entrance is closely confined by hedges as far as the grotto-like alcove on one end of an outbuilding. From here high stone walls enclose two sides of the garden and a hornbeam tunnel surrounds the other two sides, punctuated by openings at the ends and middles to display urns, seats, statues and the octagonal gazebo in the centre of the garden. The paths which parallel the walls and quarter the garden are edged with apple trees and box-lined borders filled with pinks, old roses, lilies, grey-leaved plants and innumerable other flowers with the emphasis on pink, white and mauve, including a hedge of 'Rosa Mundi'. The atmosphere owes at least as much to the Virginian origins of its creator as to any English gardening tradition.

Of the four squares in the walled garden two are now grassed, the third is a circular garden with alternate beds of iris and strawberries around a central apple tree and the fourth is a fascinating maze-like garden modelled on the Roman pavement at Torcello.

Doors from the walled garden lead to the 'back yard'. Here horticultural interest is concentrated along the walls which shelter many climbers, bulbs, and tender plants. Plain panels of grass and gravel provide a welcome contrast to the richness and a graceful setting for the modernized coach-house at one end and a delightful group of three small linked buildings at the other, a group which again reminds one of the recent formation of the garden: only two of the buildings existed before 1960.

Hatfield House, Hatfield, Herts (The Marquess of Salisbury)

50 acres; 5–6 gardeners; gravel with occasional clay pockets. Open late Mar–early Oct. *House and West Gardens:* daily except Mons, weekdays 12–5; Suns 2–5.30. Open Bank Hols and Easter Mon 11–5 but closed Good Friday. *East and West Gardens* (but not house): Mons (except Bank Hols) 2–5. See HHCG. Opposite Hatfield station.

Hatfield House, one of the major houses of the English Renaissance, is situated in a park imprinted with great avenues. Although many notable designers were associated with its development, the Cecils have always taken a close personal interest and visitors can expect to find improvements still in progress.

The Old Palace, completed in 1497 by the Bishop of Ely, was used after the Dissolution by Henry VIII. In 1558 Elizabeth I heard of her accession while reading under an oak, the remains of which can still be

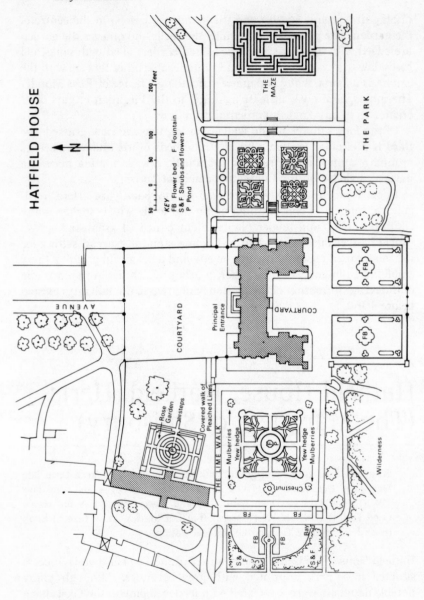

HATFIELD HOUSE

N

KEY
FB Flower bed   F Fountain
S & F Shrubs and flowers
P Pond

50 0 50 100 200 feet

THE MAZE

THE PARK

COURTYARD

Principal
Entrance

COURTYARD

AVENUE

Rose
Garden

Steps

Covered walk of
Pleached Limes

THE LIME WALK

Mulberries

Yew hedge

Yew hedge

Mulberries

Chestnut

Wilderness

FB

FB

FB

FB

FB

FB

Bay

S & F

S & F

seen on the cross-avenue north east of the house. James I preferred Robert Cecil's estate at Theobalds and in 1607 an exchange was agreed, beginning the Cecils' uninterrupted connection with Hatfield.

In 1608 Cecil, 1st Earl of Salisbury, pulled down three sides of the Old Palace and built a great new house. Elaborate terraced gardens were designed and planted from 1609–1614 by John Tradescant and Mountain Jennings with waterworks by the French engineer Salamon de Caux. In 1611 Tradescant was sent on the first of many expeditions through Europe, sending back the best fruits and flowers for the garden. 600 lime trees were sent for the avenues and it was at Hatfield that tulips and the double anemone were first seen in Britain.

The family fortunes were diminished by the spendthrift 6th Earl (1713–1780) but, good fortune restored by the 7th Earl, later 1st Marquess of Salisbury, Hatfield flourished once more in the nineteenth century. This success was reflected in the garden as well as in the house which was restored to the Jacobean style. The 2nd Marquess recreated the terraced east gardens and, in 1841, planted the famous maze. The gates to the south were erected for Queen Victoria's visit in 1846 and the West Garden was restored in 1900. Many flowering trees – cherries and crab apples especially – were planted in the 1950s and 1960s and, most recently, the 7th Marquess has rebuilt the east terrace.

The first impression at Hatfield House is of grandeur: avenues converge on the north front with its great court surrounded by elegant pierced walls. In the West Garden, however, the scale is more appropriate to the remaining side of the Old Palace, which is adjacent. The present pattern of scrolled beds and hedges, established *c*.1900, was based on the old garden of 1607. Three of the four mulberries planted by James I have declined and fallen but one remains in good condition. The lime walks, too, date back at least to the eighteenth century. From the West Garden steps descend into the Scented Garden which bears the unmistakable imprint of the Marchioness. Its planting is very reminiscent of the garden at Cranborne Manor, which the Marchioness also planted. The sundial is surrounded by herbs, a chamomile path and a hedge of sweetbriar. Herbs, fragrance, white flowers and grey foliage are much in evidence in the wide borders around the garden, while the subdivision and levels of the garden cleverly mask a four-foot drop from south to north. The planting is modern but the garden could easily have served as the Ladies' Garden for the Old Palace, such is its timeless charm.

South of the formal gardens is a Wilderness. Large beech trees, planted by the 5th Countess early in the eighteenth century, lead to tall oaks and chestnuts underplanted with cherries, rhododendrons and bulbs. Here, too, are the remains of a pinetum planted by the 2nd Marquess. From the Wilderness there are views of the south front of the house, its deep wings and green lawns providing an inviting approach. The gates erected for Queen Victoria remain but most of the flower beds characteristic of that age have disappeared.

The East Garden is open only on Mondays, when the house is closed, but is worth a special visit. In the eighteenth century the terraces and parterres were swept away and the garden remained landscaped until formality was restored by the 2nd Marquess. The terrace and square garden below the house have been restored recently. *Quercus ilex* for the walks and statuary on the steps were brought from Italy in 1974. From the square garden, paths descend to the croquet lawn and thence to the maze. Below the swimming pool garden on the next level, paths on either side curve between cherries and magnolias around the informal margins of the 'New Pond'. A large *Zelkova* and *Malus sargentii* are among many plants remaining from the 1876 shrubbery, and clearings for magnolias, embothriums and other exciting plants promise continued interest.

Not least of the attractions of this quiet part of the garden is the fine reflection in the pond of the east façade of the house framed by informal trees.

Heronsgate Gardens, Rickmansworth, Herts

3–4 gardens in Long Lane open for Red Cross once in Sept, including *Lady Walk* – 2 acres, ½ gardener; *Sherwood* – 2 acres, no gardener; soil, clay cap over chalk. Heronsgate is signposted from roundabout on North Orbital road (A412) ½ mile E of Rickmansworth.

Heronsgate was a Chartist settlement laid out in 1847 to create a new rural way of life for its members. The scheme foundered but the community still provides a pleasant environment and some interesting gardens.

Lady Walk is a newer house (1936) on the edge of the estate, with formal gardens and excellent views. The drive leads up to a low-walled forecourt, the house on the left, a new swimming pool garden opposite and, continuing the line of the drive, imposing semi-circular steps into the garden. The hillside is terraced into rectangular gardens with handsome steps, walls and paths at the lower level leading to a formal rose garden and a long herbaceous border along the wall concealing the kitchen garden. The designer is unknown but was clearly very able.

These small gardens lead to open lawn and informal shrub planting masking the tennis court while a long terrace on the south front looks across to distant hills. Behind the tennis court the boundary is formed by native trees with a derelict orchard now being replanted.

Sherwood, only two houses away, is in another world. It is one of the original houses and its garden is a model of good Victorian planning, simple in outline yet varied in content. The house is in the south corner and the drive, following the north-east boundary for much of its length, crosses to divide the garden in two. The small east corner has a small rose garden surrounded, almost engulfed, by large rhododendrons and a cedar. It is dark and cool, in contrast to the larger part which consists of open lawn enclosed on two sides by trees fringing the drive and public road, and on the third by a raised walk and yew hedge concealing the vegetable garden.

Much of the garden is being simplified, and will be better for it, but between the vegetable garden and the house is a new garden designed in 1973. Gently mounded grass partly conceals a paved corner surrounded by banks of shrubs, many planted for foliage and ground cover. Stepping stones emphasize the curves of the land form and lead to the swimming pool with its twin pavilions framing the axis of the vegetable garden. In the choice of plants, incorporation of existing features (especially a picturesque apple tree) and use of land form to create privacy without complete enclosure, this is a delightful addition to a very pleasant garden.

Hexton Manor, Hexton, Herts

---

36 acres; 2 gardeners; clay soil. Open once in July for RC etc. On B655 between Hitchin (6 miles) and Barton in the Clay (2 miles).

The reduction of the garden staff to two and the necessity to concentrate on the semi-commercial kitchen garden mean that there is little time to spare on flower gardens, but the surroundings of the eighteenth-century manor-house are peaceful and attractive.

A long beech drive follows the boundary from Pegsdon Lodge with occasional views over the upper lake. The drive forks, winding around a little secret garden to the house on the right and leading between short lime avenues to the stables and three kitchen gardens on the left. Two of these are still used, with well-trained plums on the walls and fine old glasshouses.

The main garden was created by Joseph Andrew de Lautour *c.*1830 with three lakes separated by cascades and decorated with bridges and gothic summerhouses. The lower lakes and the buildings are now neglected but there is much to interest the keen garden explorer, and a new border of pillar roses and herbaceous plants was started in 1974.

Hill House, Stanstead Abbots, Herts

7 acres; 1 gardener; gravel and sand with springs. Open once in June for RC. From Hertford, follow A414 almost through Stanstead Abbots then fork left into Cappell Lane.

To describe a patch of hawthorn and dog roses as a major feature of a garden does not sound very flattering but at Hill House it can be said without denigrating the rest of this charming garden. Hawthorn scrub on the edge of an older wood has been skilfully cleared to form a glade scattered with dog roses and backed by rising ground, a fine example of when to leave well alone. When carpeted with fritillaries and cowslips in the spring it must be counted a major feature.

From the walled gardens, now used as aviaries, a path leads around the orchard towards the house but a better route is through the glade to a narrow woodland path around a small valley of snowdrops and primroses. The path emerges suddenly from a clump of mahonia to reveal the water garden. Here a series of small pools belies the sandy soil while small trees, shrubs, ferns and waterside plants create a luxuriant atmosphere. Primulas, meconopsis and foxgloves thrive alongside native orchids.

The main part of the garden, horticulturally speaking, is on higher land sloping more uniformly and gently to the west of the house. A steep drive shaded by plane trees leads to an open, rose-bordered lawn from which there are distant views. The conservatory, walls and

1. Ascott: the pool and lively sculpture, surrounded by seasonal bedding, is a fitting terminus to the formal gardens. Outside the yew hedges the garden is informal with clipped beech and yew to link formality and informality.

2. Blenheim: the water parterre designed by Achille Duchêne creates an impressive foreground to one of Lancelot Brown's finest landscape parks.

3. Brook Cottage: surrounded by a luxuriant combination of foliage textures and colours, the pond occupies an important position between the older terraced garden and more extensive new garden around the tennis court.

4. Broughton Castle: informal borders around the box-hedged fleurs-de-lis occupy the site of former kitchens. The effectiveness of this charming garden is enhanced by the surprise which attends its discovery.

5. Buscot Park: this grand stairway linking the forecourt and extensive walled gardens is one of many formal vistas in the garden designed mainly by Harold Peto.

6. Cliveden: the great parterre, once a masterpiece of Victorian bedding, has been restored by the National Trust. Box, santolina and senecio pick out the pattern and avoid the necessity of expensive seasonal planting.

7. Cliveden: the water garden has been opened up and extended in recent years, much to its advantage. Many bulbs and good ground-cover plants are included in the new perimeter planting.

8. Compton Beauchamp: the effect of this long herbaceous border is greatly enhanced by the contrasting deep shade at either end. A paeony garden, rose garden, winter garden and moat are other features of the garden.

9. Cornwell Manor: good architecture softened, not obliterated, by good planting characterizes Cornwell Manor. These steps head up to the swimming pool with roses, lavender and lilies on all sides.

10. Fanhams Hall: the centrepiece of the rose-garden, a huge lotus bowl, provides a link with the Japanese garden beyond. Sheltered borders below the steps accommodate many interesting, unusual and rather tender plants.

11. Hatfield House: a walk around the 'old pond' offers an unusual view of Hatfield House. Bordering the walk are many interesting plants of this century and last.

12. Hatfield House: the yew-hedged herbaceous garden, based on the plan of a much older garden on this site, is seen here framed by the lime walk.

14. Luton Hoo: the development of a garden centre at Luton Hoo has made possible the restoration of this long glasshouse range. Its contents recreate much of the splendour of the palm house in its heyday.

13. Hill End Farm Cottage, Leverstock Green: this new, small garden is given much added interest by careful use of foliage and paving textures, not least around this arched entrance from the car port.

15. Luton Hoo: the rock-work, concealed from the landscape parkland around it, is impressive in scale. The cavern seen here is but a small part of the whole scheme.

16. Milton Manor: the setting of Milton Manor among several fine trees is simple and dignified. A nearby walled garden has been partially redeveloped as a more intimate pleasure garden.

17. Nuneham: a whole village was removed from the environs of Nuneham to create this picturesque scene. The classical 'temple' which replaced the village church dominates several vistas within the garden.

18. Old Rectory, Farnborough: the shrub-rose garden of the Old Rectory has all the best qualities of modern gardening—firm outlines, flowing planting and restrained use of colour.

19. Pusey House: the main path down from the house crosses the water by a spreading Oriental Plane. A small part of the richly-planted waterside garden can just be seen to left and right of the bridge.

Rousham: renowned as a William Kent landscape, Rousham also has
ny features of more horticultural interest, not least of which is this
x-hedged rose garden near the pigeon house.

21. Savill Gardens, Windsor Great Park: raised alpine beds of simple shape provide a useful example for much smaller gardens where fake mountain scenery is quite inappropriate. The wall in the background supports climbers and shelters many tender plants.

22. Steart Hill House: roses provide the main interest at Steart Hill but many other plants are used to create and supplement colour schemes. A dip in the bank of tall shrub roses allows views across the ha-ha from the main rose garden.

23. Stowe: soft haze emphasizes the grand simplicity of Bridgeman's plan at Stowe, subsequently softened in outline to make perhaps the most famous English landscape garden.

24. Westfields: elegant formality here merges into informal glades and rockwork in other parts of this garden designed by Percy Cane. Pools, statuary and evergreen planting create a permanent framework for the garden.

25. West Wycombe Park: Revett's 'Music Temple' occupies an important position in the landscape of West Wycombe. New planting is intended to screen undesirable intrusions and to retain the scale of this small gem of eighteenth century design.

26. Wexham Springs: concrete is put to many uses around the Cement and Concrete Association's research station. Here a simple two-tone pattern adds breadth to a very long path.

buildings shelter many interesting plants but the greatest floral interest lies beyond the gate into the present kitchen garden.

Although not walled, the quartered plan is evident. The main borders, predominantly yellow and purple, terminate at a seat shaded by yew. The cross walk is lined in the lower part with apples and paeonies, screening a wilderness of cherries, buddleias and lilacs. In the upper part, a quincunx of *Pyrus salicifolia* 'Pendula' blends with the newest border of blue and white.

Elsewhere, alstroemerias, strawberries and cabbages each have their place in a delightful mixture of flowers, fruit and vegetables.

Hollycroft and Holly Meadow, Knebworth, Herts

Open once in May for RC. In Deards End Lane, Old Knebworth.

These two nearby gardens share the flat terrain and gravel soil of the district but are otherwise quite different in character making interesting comparisons.

Hollycroft (3 acres; $\frac{1}{2}$ gardener) is an open garden in which borders of 'Peace' roses leading to a sunken garden and informal pool create a central colourful feature. A rose-lined walk curves around two sides to frame views of the centrepiece and apple trees beyond the walk combine beauty with utility, not only by fruiting but in screening a productive vegetable garden in one corner.

Holly Meadow (1 acre; $\frac{1}{2}$ gardener) is a garden of many enclosures, within an encompassing holly hedge planted in 1905 when the house was built. The garden is divided along its length by a pergola and yew hedge then divided across to create four main compartments. The first has twin shrub borders to echo the long border by the drive; the second is a kitchen garden near the garage, attractively screened by espalier fruit and an herbaceous border; the third is a former tennis lawn now bordered by birch, flowering trees and bulbs while the fourth, a rose garden near the house, has been diversified with hydrangeas and *Lilium regale*. A pool and small sunken garden at the end of the house lead again to the front drive, where levels have been varied to include a rock bank and shallow pool for birds.

Hook Norton Manor, Hook Norton, Oxon

4 acres; $\frac{1}{2}$ gardener; alkaline clay-loam, heavier in valley bottom. Open once or twice each year for NGS. 8 miles SW of Banbury, 2 miles N of A361 (Banbury–Chipping Norton).

The attractive appearance of Hook Norton Manor is much enhanced by its walled forecourt, smothered in a variety of climbing and trailing plants. The larger drive-cum-stable-yard to the west is the more usual entrance. A young lime forms its centrepiece and the walls again support climbers and wall shrubs. South of the house the steep slope is terraced to create two more walled enclosures, the upper one of herbaceous borders and the lower one of roses.

Pleasant though these are, the main interest of the present owners lies to the west and south on the natural slope. Below the yard, two old borders of shrubs on the upper slope have been supplemented with good foliage plants to form a small informal garden around a handsome *Liriodendron*. Since 1968 the steeper slope has been thickly planted with willows, poplars, redwoods and Holm Oaks, all of which have grown rapidly to create a jungle which is already being thinned.

The lower slope is more open with shrubby dogwoods among old apples and pears. A pond and the small stream flowing through the garden form the nucleus of a water garden which, with the tree-covered slope, constitute a wild garden increasing in interest year by year.

Howard's House, Cardington, Beds

4 acres; 1 gardener; sandy soil. Open once in April and June for GS, NGS. 2 miles SE of Bedford, off A603 (Bedford–Sandy).

Howard's House is on one edge of its large, flat, walled garden but the well-managed contrast of short and long grass reduces its scale to pleasing proportions. A wide panel of short grass occupies the central axis from the house to an old oak. Long grass on either side is planted with a wide variety of shrubs and trees, old and new.

Above a circular rose garden near the house is a memorial vase to the philanthropist, John Howard, who planted a garden here in 1762. The whole south-facing wall is covered with tender wall plants: *Piptanthus, Ceanothus, Solanum crispum, Sophora tetraptera* and many more, while across the garden, by the kitchen garden wall, is a cherry avenue, particularly beautiful in spring. The kitchen garden itself has been modified in a most attractive way. A swimming pool and large lawn have displaced most of the central vegetable plot. Vegetables are still grown in the long side borders and in beds at either end of the lawn, concealed by rugosa rose and artichoke hedges. Fruit cages against the end walls have decorative finials while the long walls carry fan-trained fruit, with a neatly trained clematis on each buttress: a delightful exception to the dereliction and disarray found in so many old walled gardens.

Hughenden Manor, High Wycombe, Bucks (The National Trust)

3 acres in 169 acres of woods and park; 1 gardener; thin chalk soil. Open Feb–Oct, every weekday except Mon and Tues, 2–6 (or sunset if earlier); Sat and Sun, 12.30–6 or sunset. See HHCG. On W side of A4128 between High Wycombe (1½ miles) and Great Missenden (6 miles).

Hughenden Manor was bought and rebuilt by Benjamin Disraeli in 1847. He lived there until his death in 1881 and it is his house which most people come to see.

The garden, much loved by Mr and Mrs Disraeli, is now modest but charming. The forecourt is an oval of grass surrounded by banks. One bank, clothed with ivy, conceals the drive as it passes in front of the house to the kitchens (now the National Trust Regional Office). The south garden, by contrast is on a ridge commanding fine views into the broad valley. Gravel walks around the lawn descend by steps and ramps into the trees. The garden once extended far into the woods and some woodland walks remain, overgrown with yews and occasionally edged with box.

The legacy of dark conifers, carpets of ivy and a few well-sited flower beds are reminders of a more colourful past and there are tentative plans to restore the garden as it is shown in photographs taken towards the end of Disraeli's life.

Hurst Lodge, Hurst, Berks

3 acres; 2 gardeners; gravel. Open once in May, once in Aug/Sept for NGS. 6 miles E of Reading on A321 opposite Hurst village pond.

There are three separate gardens at Hurst Lodge, four if one adds the wealth of climbing plants on the house itself.

By the drive, the old kitchen garden walls have been reduced to reveal a pleasure garden with wide borders of many interesting plants. The low pavilion houses a swimming pool and provides a tropical atmosphere in which ferns, bromeliads and other exotics flourish. The new and productive kitchen garden is approached beneath a gallery linking two of the three wings of the very attractive old house.

The main garden is a flat, broadly triangular lawn enclosed by fine trees and shrubs from earlier generations of this gardening family, with many smaller plants added by the present owner. At the entrance to this part of the garden is a little knot of clipped box filled with bright flowers while against the far boundary is a yellow border, another bright spot against the deep shadows of cedar, beech and sycamore. Shrubs planted within the boundary form centres of island beds filled with shrub roses, ferns, lilies and innumerable other plants while paths wind through sun and shade. *Polygonum filiforme* (*Tovara virginiana*), a rarely seen but delightful plant, brightens many a dark corner here and the golden *Weigela looymansii* 'Aurea' spreads sunshine on the dullest days.

The apex of the triangle is newly planted with varied trees. On the third side of the triangle a heather mound forms a conspicuous feature. Much nearer the house is a shadowy pond overhung by a splendid scarlet oak. Almost hiding the nearby gate to the vegetable garden is a magnificent pine jostling with a balsam poplar. The poplar was planted in 1952 in anticipation of the pine's demise, but the latter has yet to fall!

Ibstone House, Ibstone, Bucks

4 acres; part-time gardener; acid sandy soil over chalk. Open once in April for GS. At S end of Ibstone, midway between Thame and Henley-on-Thames. 2 miles S of Exit 5 from M40.

Ibstone House stands by the road, on a narrow ridge with extensive views across the valley to the east. William Robinson laid out the garden after sweeping the lawn free of the remnants of an older garden, and most of the planting dates from 1864 to 1900 when cedars, firs and pines were planted. Dame Cicely Andrews lived here from 1940 to 1968. Since 1970 much of the laurel has been cleared to reveal the outlines of the garden.

Opposite the wisteria-clad west façade, weeping holly and double pink hawthorn serve as reminders of a Victorian legacy, as does a picturesque but ageing weeping *Aesculus x carnea* on the lawn. A shaded walk beneath large trees on the west boundary continues around the tennis court to return along a retaining wall above the steep slope. Rhododendrons have been cut back, and a small rose garden and new trees added to rejuvenate the garden.

Steep steps bordered by tree paeonies descend the grass slope to the kitchen garden with its herbaceous border and sheltered summerhouse against the outer wall. Within, half the walled garden is still cultivated. The grass slope between upper and lower gardens is thick with bulbs, wild flowers and *Tellima* among circles of fruit trees, a characteristic Robinson planting. The large Cedar of Lebanon, planted to commemorate Wesley's preaching here, survives from the older garden layout.

Jasmine House, Hatch Bridge, Berks

¼ acre; no help; neutral sandy loam. Open once in May for NGS. 2 miles W of Windsor on A308 (Windsor–Maidenhead) opposite entrance to Windsor Marina.

Jasmine House was built in 1956 in a cul-de-sac around a small copse. The wedge-shaped plot has the advantage of a small frontage looking onto the copse and a much wider private garden behind the house. The garden has developed since 1962 as the main interest of a keen amateur gardener. As the flat field beyond offers more exposure to east winds than attractive prospect, the boundary is being enclosed by hollies and rugosa roses so interest is focused within the garden.

In front of the house a rose border is being replaced by azaleas, hydrangeas and other plants more in keeping with the overall character of the garden. The north boundary, too, (one of the first borders to be planted) is being replanted to reflect changed interests. The house itself supports a group of ivies, especially useful in winter, and the path is lined with sink and trough gardens.

South of the house, raised beds and a pool have been formed, over the original stable paviors. Separating drive and garden is a wooden shelter designed by the owner for his bonsai.

The east garden, much wider than deep, has been developed as a series of island beds. Heathers, conifers, azaleas, dwarf bulbs and decorative barked trees make the garden attractive throughout the year, but it is the careful arrangement of these plants which lifts this garden out of the ordinary. A statue in the south-east corner, seen from many angles among the planting, terminates an uninterrupted vista along the east boundary while a small pool to the north is almost concealed within roses and other shrubs. The contrasts of island beds, open vista and secluded pool make the garden seem far larger than it really is.

Juniper Hill, Penn, Bucks

$3\frac{1}{2}$ acres; 1 gardener; acid clay-loam over chalk. Open Sun and Mon of Spring Bank Hol then one weekend later in year, for NGS. Plant sales. Penn is in centre of Amersham–Beaconsfield–High Wycombe triangle. From B474 turn S at Slade's Garage, then $\frac{1}{2}$ mile on left.

To rebuild a house for the sake of a view sounds an extreme measure, but the rebuilding of Juniper Hill in 1958 was amply justified by the magnificent vista thus obtained from the highest part of Beacon Hill. The view is well matched by an interesting garden.

South of the drive natural springs supply a water garden, a series of small pools descending between irises, primulas and other marginal plants. Beyond this secluded garden, along the south front of the house is a terrace from which the view is framed between tall cypresses terminating a double border. Shrubs, roses, paeonies and other plants provide a long season of interest and, although most people will see the borders in the summer, it is worth examining the way in which evergreen shrubs have been grouped to conceal rose stems and provide winter interest.

Shrub roses, rhododendrons, camellias and hydrangeas play important parts in the island borders increasing in height from the central vista to the woodland edged with Japanese azaleas. Within the woodland, more demanding plants are grown. In the borders edged with oak logs and heavily mulched with leaf-mould there are many fine rhododendrons, lilies, primulas and foliage plants. Spring bulbs are later concealed by hostas and ferns.

In the greenhouse and frames below the woodland garden, many plants are successfully propagated to be sold for charity.

Kings Copse House, Southend, Reading, Berks

2 acres plus 30 acres woodland; 1 gardener; gravel soil. Open once in June for GS. 9 miles W of Reading. Midway between Bradfield and Bucklebury turn S for ½ mile beyond Standford Dingley.

Kings Copse House is set on a gravel hilltop with extensive views over woodland and farmland to the west.

Of the Edwardian garden, there remains a broad stone-flagged walk along the south front of the house continuing along an herbaceous border at the upper end of the kitchen garden, while the wall screening the kitchen garden from view has its western exposure exploited by *Carpenteria*, Tree Paeonies, *Solanum crispum* and other interesting shrubs. Rose beds and a pool remain from the more complicated design of a formal garden while the lawn beyond slopes to a second more secluded rose garden.

It is the woodland, however, which provides the main attraction. Rhododendrons and azaleas form outlying groups for the woodland proper, and are echoed by similar plantings in the scattered clearings in the woods. Snowdrops, bluebells, orchids and many other wild flowers carpet the wooded slopes while tall Canadian Balsam competes successfully with brambles in the moist, flatter areas.

Kingsmoor, Sunningdale, Berks

8 acres; 1 gardener; Bagshot sand. Open once in May for NGS. From A30 in Sunningdale, take Chobham and Woking road, then first right after railway bridge (Titlark's Hill).

When Kingsmoor was built in 1910, the garden was made by John Waterer and Sons. After a period of neglect from 1960 to 1965 it has now been restored. It is encouraging to note not only the improved condition of the garden but also the many new plants replacing shrubs and trees now nearing the end of their life-span.

The house is in the north-east corner, well sited to exploit the slight slope across the garden's short axis to the south, and the house and garden are closely linked. To the west is a small formal garden with herbaceous plants against the sunny wall, and hydrangeas in the shade. To the south, a wisteria-clad portico opens onto a terrace and thus to the main vista between high banks of shrubs to a rose garden. The yew hedge around this was cut back to the trunks in 1971–74 to re-shape it.

Below the terrace, walks lead to the left and right. To the left is the swimming pool and greenhouse above the croquet lawn. To the right a curving laburnum avenue passes below the formal garden to the main open lawn, irregular in shape and bordered by birch, hydrangeas, rhododendrons and *Liquidambar*. A catalpa is the main central feature, with new beds of heaths and conifers. New birch and azaleas supplement older plants to conceal a delightful 'lawn' of Ling (*Calluna vulgaris*), separated in turn from the vegetable garden by an avenue of cherries leading back to the rose garden and croquet lawn.

The garden is always attractive. In spring there are azaleas, cherries and other flowering trees. In summer, roses and annuals take their place among the varied greens of many maples and other interesting shrubs which then colour brilliantly in the autumn. In winter there are evergreens, ornamental bark and the overall design. That this is now maintained by one gardener is quite remarkable.

Kingstone Lisle Park, Wantage, Oxon

31 acres plus lakes; $5\frac{1}{2}$ gardeners (2 in pleasure garden); thin soil over chalk. Open once in April and June for NGS. 5 miles W of Wantage, N of B4507 (Wantage–Swindon).

Kingstone Lisle House has a large, open garden with a rather complex layout, the more so because the house was altered to make the entrance on the north instead of the south side. The modern drive passes between the parish church and entrance lodge in a wide sweep to the forecourt north of the house. On the right is an irregular walled kitchen garden (a commercial enterprise) and on the left is an extensive area of shrubs in grass, with the park and lakes below.

The low walls of the forecourt continue east of the house to the south front where they surround a sunken octagonal pool. The open boundary allows uninterrupted views down to the lake. Above the old drive, still clearly evident, the natural slope is divided by a screen of pleached limes and trained apples into a series of rectangular lawns, formerly vegetable gardens. Nearer the house, the slope is terraced to admit a croquet lawn, rose garden and tennis court.

The walled garden contains several greenhouses producing mainly carnations, tomatoes and pot plants, but one house still has arches of trained peaches along the central pathway, a most unusual and interesting remnant of the original kitchen garden.

Kingston House, Kingston Bagpuize, Oxon

30 acres; 2 gardeners; limestone soil. Open every Mon between April and Sept for NGS and garden upkeep. 5½ miles W of Abingdon near crossing of A415 and A420.

Kingston House, built in 1670, was 'turned around' in the 1850s and the drive now winds around to a small forecourt on the west front, enclosed by two fine Cut-leaved Beech. The east front has an open lawn bordered by gravel walks with four tall Wellingtonias framing the view over the ha-ha to a beech avenue some distance away. The lawn is enclosed on both sides but the orientation is interesting in that the stables and kitchen garden are to the south and the pleasure garden to the north, the reverse of the normal arrangement for houses of this date.

A shrub border conceals the stables but there is a second sunken path alongside the stables from which to view the camellias and other shrubs in this shaded corner. The lawn north of the house, broken by occasional conifers, is bordered on two sides by walls which support and shelter a wide range of plants. There are borders of herbaceous plants and bearded iris, wall shrubs and paeonies. Part of the wall is not free standing but supports a raised walk which appears to be much older than the house. From this walk there is a view over the most important part of the garden.

About an acre between the curving drive and the house has been developed since 1945 as a woodland garden. Despite the alkaline nature of the original soil it now contains an enormous range of bulbs, shrubs and woodland plants. Except for the central vista only narrow winding paths interrupt the continuous carpet of plants, many of which are quite rare. An old evergreen hedge on the east side has been thinned but still encloses the garden from the open field. In the field, carefully sited to be seen from the entrance and from near the house, there is a large border of shrubs and dwarf conifers and groups of varied trees, the most recent extension of the garden.

Since 1939 the garden has been developed by Miss Raphael who, for 30 years until her death in 1976, was the organiser of National Gardens Scheme in Berkshire and the Vale of the White Horse. Her niece, who inherited the property, shares a love of gardening and, although changes are inevitable to reflect the new owner's interests, this will continue to be a most interesting garden.

Knebworth House, Stevenage, Herts (Lytton Enterprises Ltd.)

---

5 acres; 3 gardeners; sandy soil. Open daily, except Mons, April–Sept, then Suns only in October. Also open Bank Hol Mons. See HHCG. 1 mile S of Stevenage, signposted from A1(M) at Stevenage.

Most visitors to Knebworth come to the Country Park or to see the house, home of the Lyttons since 1492, but the gardens should not be overlooked. The present garden at Knebworth, a formal design of pleached limes, yew hedges and lawns, is the work of Edwin Lutyens and it had personal significance for him: in 1897 he married Lady Emily Lytton in Knebworth church. The garden also contains many trees from an older, more elaborate layout.

The main feature of the garden is, of course, the house. The fantasy of stuccoed turrets and battlements was plastered onto the remaining wing of the original Tudor brick quadrangle in 1811–1816 and extensively refurbished in 1843. Stables and yards occupy the north side of the house. Wide gravel paths skirt the south and west sides giving splendid close views of the house and, from the 'mounts', more distant views of Knebworth church and the park. On the east side, the original Tudor front, lies the garden proper.

Limes border an open sunken lawn and small pool, echoing the lines of a sixteenth-century garden in much simplified form. Beyond the limes is a rose garden flanked by herbaceous borders and backed by a semi-circular yew hedge with wings extending to answer the house. Statues stand out against the dark yew, and a narrow opening leads through to another alcove with a small pool and buttressed yew hedges on three sides.

From this point the garden remains only in sketchy outline, terminating in the low raised bank of a former terrace with a small maze in one corner. The wide cross path which separated the lime walks and rose garden, and on which visitors enter the garden, continues between impressive mounds of a former rock garden to a quiet backwater of orchard and yew trees with herbaceous borders against the walls of the kitchen garden.

Leggatts Park, Potters Bar, Herts

16 acres garden and paddock with 40 acres woodland; 1 gardener; gravel soil. Open once in late May or June for RC. On E side of A1000 N of Little Heath; midway between Potters Bar and Bell Bar.

The Victorian character of Leggatts Park, immediately apparent when one enters the drive bordered by alternate pairs of cedars and redwoods, is confirmed on reaching the house. A picturesque rustic porch shelters the north entrance while, on the south front, an octagonal conservatory overlooks winding walks around a small group of conifers. The house was, in fact, built in 1833 as a farmhouse but considerably enlarged and the garden formed in 1886.

Other features are more recent in origin. The rose garden west of the main lawn, on the site of a former kitchen garden, the elaborate sunken garden, to the east and the overgrown rock garden on the south slope, designed by Waterers, date from about 1930 when there was a change of ownership. The swimming pool is even more recent (c.1970).

The interest and Victorian influence is not confined to the immediate environs of the house. To the east, beyond the rose garden and present vegetable garden, a formal walk bordered by alternate rhododendrons and hollies crosses the field to the woodland boundary whence walks diverge through birch, rhododendrons and bluebells, returning eventually to the drive or farmyard.

The woods and farm are also open to visitors on this one day.

Leverstock Green Gardens

Three gardens open once in July for GS; displays of flower arrangements. From St Albans (4 miles) turn right into Westwick Row by corner farm after M1 new bridge. From Hemel Hempstead turn left down Pancake Lane after Leverstock Green church then turn right at 'T' junction.

These three gardens are as different in character as one could imagine and together make a stimulating day's visit especially as the attractive Tudor houses are also open to display flower arrangements by one of the owners.

Westwick Cottage ($2\frac{1}{2}$ acres; part-time help), once a row of four cottages, has a wide brick path along its front leading to a secluded brick patio. Its owner was a close associate of the late Constance Spry and, not surprisingly, the garden is filled with plants of value in flower arranging. The wide border along the path features the shrub rose 'Constance Spry' and, with a long curving border around the boundary, encloses an irregular lawn. Both borders are filled with shrubs, herbaceous plants, annuals, bulbs and grasses. Across the drive is a more shaded area of small island beds and small trees. Heathers, rhododendrons and a small rock garden each have their own islands but foliage shrubs, lilies, spurges, hostas, hellebores and many other plants are planted freely throughout the area. Behind the house is a small vegetable garden and orchard.

King Charles II Cottage (1 acre; weekend help), only yards away, is a complete contrast. Here the brick is whitewashed in crisp contrast to the black beams and the garden is a model of neatness and order. The drive bisects the garden in a long curve. On one side, from the wide stone terrace, is a deep border of azaleas and roses with an edging of low bedding plants. Beyond the drive a fallen apple tree, still growing well, forms a picturesque focal point near a small pool almost concealed under a willow. A beech hedge leads to a tiny sheltered brick corner. Some hedge plants died but, as they were conveniently near the middle, the opportunity was seized to make an arch focusing back towards the house and an ancient sundial, rescued from obscurity on the rubbish-heap of a Scottish inn.

Hill End Farm Cottage ($\frac{1}{16}$ acre; no help), nearly a mile away, is perhaps the most remarkable of the three gardens especially when one considers that it has been created since 1971 on a then bare, windswept hillside. The scheme of the garden is very simple but its interesting details make it a garden of immense charm.

A single curving border follows the entire irregular boundary. Near the road is a forest of delphinium spikes in early summer. A wrought iron gate leads from the gravelled drive through a rose-covered brick arch to a narrow, intricately patterned path of bricks, stone and concrete slabs. This widens to form an irregular terrace around the sunnier walls of the house. The framed entrance, finely textured pattern of the paving softened by trailing plants and decorated with stone sinks creates a deceptively spacious feeling, emphasized by the contrast between open lawn and densely planted border. The border encloses and shelters the garden more each year, counterbalancing the slope of the lawn. Yellow plants predominate: Golden Privet, *Weigela, Robinia,* and *Alchemilla* and the flowers of roses, *Thalictrum* and *Hypericum* create their own sunshine in all weathers.

A row of *Cupressus macrocarpa* existing before 1971 has been retained to create a concealed back garden. Its purpose is to accommodate the washing line but it also serves as an intimate and very attractive garden-in-a-garden.

Lime Close, Drayton, Oxon

3½ acres; ½ gardener; soil fertile alkaline loam over chalk. Open once in spring for NGS. 2 miles S of Abingdon. On E side of B4017 in Drayton, turn into Henley's Lane by Rogowski's newsagent.

Until 1967 Lime Close had a large but crowded collection of small ornamental trees. Between 1967 and 1972 over 100 trees were removed and many shrubs were propagated ready for planting. Considerable care has been taken to propagate only good forms of the many interesting shrubs used.

Despite drastic thinning many of the best trees have been left to furnish the garden which is now enriched with shrubs, herbaceous plants, bulbs and, most important, enough open space to display the plants well.

A rose garden by the entrance borders a wide gravel drive which continues along the house to raised beds. Their dry walls were rebuilt in 1973/4 and now house many interesting low plants. The lawn is fringed with small trees thickening over a 'woodland' border at one end and opening to the small kitchen garden at the other.

Beyond the public footpath the informal planting continues using many plants moved from elsewhere in the garden. A small pool has been made and a belt of oak seedlings is gradually replacing the many large elms which have died.

A long herbaceous border on the east boundary and an all-season border on the south are more formal. The latter, seen from the breakfast table, is rarely without flowers. The herbaceous border has an increasing complement of shrubs, with climbers on the stone wall behind.

Near the house is a flourishing alpine house by a tufa bank planted in 1976. At the other end of the house a vigorous young *Parrotia* conceals the path back into the rose garden at the entrance.

Little Bowden, Pangbourne, Berks

12 acres; 1 gardener; acid sandy soil. Open once in May for NGS. 1½ miles W of Pangbourne on S side of road to Ashampstead and Yattendon.

The garden of Little Bowden is in three interconnected parts. East and immediately south of the house, a paved garden and formal pool enclosed by yew hedges are contemporary with the house (1906–8).

Shallow brick steps south of the pool lead to a beautiful glade in the oak wood, carpeted with bluebells, bordered by rhododendrons planted in 1930 and subsequently enriched with azaleas, hydrangeas and magnolias planted since 1950 when the glade was restored. A meandering path returns through wilder woodland and crosses an informal pool to the open lawn. It is worth noting here the plants used to create a 'waterside' luxuriance in what is in fact a very dry position. *Aruncus*, paeonies, spurges and hellebores are especially evident.

The garden east of the house is more recent. Here the path winds round a concealed tennis court to an area of island beds, small trees and bulbs. Grey and copper foliage and roses are important, particularly in the border by the yew hedge concealing the vegetables. The old hedge is from 1930, the newer section enclosing the swimming pool, from 1961. There are many interesting plants on the sheltered wall of the pool garden and on the pergola leading from it, while a 'Bobby James' rose scrambles through an old apple to screen this side of the tennis court.

By the pergola is a cutting garden which, with most other parts of the garden, provides a steady supply of flowers for making dried arrangements.

Little Heath Farm, Potten End, Herts

---

2 acre nursery plus 1 acre garden; 4 staff (garden maintained by owner); clay and gravel patches over chalk. Open once in May, June and Sept for NGS. Nursery open during business hours. $1\frac{1}{2}$ miles NE of Berkhamsted. From A41 turn N at Bourne End church.

At Little Heath Farm, three activities are proceeding simultaneously: the restoration of a derelict seventeenth-century farmhouse, the development of a garden from the wasteland around it and the establishment of a nursery from which many of the interesting plants grown in the garden are distributed. Ducks, chickens and other live-stock also add interest, especially for children, when the garden is open.

The main garden is being developed around the clay-lined pond, between the drive, the farm buildings and a tall hedgerow, so within the space of much less than an acre the situation varies from open, sunny grass to dry shade, from waterside to the sun-baked rubble heap by the outbuildings. The range of plants is equally varied but special interest is shown in good foliage plants, especially variegated ones, cottage garden plants and the less common herbaceous and ground-cover plants. In addition to the main garden, which is beginning to extend around the farmhouse and into the adjacent field, there is a rock garden within the nursery area to extend the range of interest still further.

1 Cliveden: the herbaceous border designed by Graham Thomas is in bright yellows and reds. Note the grouping of plants in flower at this time, with earlier and later flowering plants forming the green foreground and background of the border

2 North Mymms Park: a magnificent rose garden is the principal garden feature at North Mymms. Thyme, candytuft, veronica and other crevice plants soften the formality of its stone paths

3 Old Vicarage, Bucklebury: soft, informal planting within firm outlines, seen here in the herb garden of the Old Vicarage, characterizes the garden as a whole. *Vitis coignetiae* on the potting shed almost conceals the orchid houses in the kitchen garden

4 Shinfield Grange: birch, witch-hazel and other autumn-colouring plants are also attractive in winter and spring. The informal planting bordering this winding walk conceals a more formal rose garden for summer display

Little Paston, Fulmer, Bucks

10 acres; 2 gardeners; acid sandy soil. Open twice in May, for GS and NGS. In Fulmer Common Road, 4 miles N of Slough in triangle formed by A40, A332 and A412.

Little Paston was built in 1929 as a small replica of Paston House in Norfolk. Developed from a wilderness of birch and *Rhododendron ponticum*, the garden was originally part of Langley Park, and a carriage drive encircling the garden has been retained to ease mechanized maintenance. Most of the garden has been developed since 1955 with major additions in 1971. The design is such that, despite the large size of the garden, its extreme flatness is no disadvantage.

The large lawn within the drive is fringed with irregular borders of rhododendrons and heathers with a deep mixed border along the western edge. Most plants are labelled. Between drive and boundary, the rhododendrons have been left as a background but the boundary belt is wide enough to have been hollowed for further interest.

West of the entrance is a small lawn with young trees: *Metasequoia*, *Liquidambar* etc. This is linked by narrow paths through the rhododendrons to a long water garden opening to a pool and summerhouse looking back to the house. On the east side, a large bed of species roses, much overgrown, was cut to the ground in 1973 and is now flourishing again. Deeper into the shade are new rhododendrons, especially larger leaved and more tender types. A raised seat in this corner has been so sited that, from its elevated position the eye ranges over apparently endless undulating planting. This vista was made even more extensive by carefully thinning the south boundary to reveal large old rhododendron cultivars in adjacent property.

In the north-east corner is the kitchen garden, enclosed on two sides by rhododendrons and concealed from the main garden by the house and swimming pool pavilion, linked by a rhododendron hedge backing an herbaceous border.

Luton Hoo, Luton, Beds (Lady Wernher)

10 acres in 1,500-acre park; 4 gardeners; clay soil. Open mid-April to mid-July, Wed, Thurs and Bank Hol Mon, 11–6; late July–Sept, Mon, Wed, Thurs and Sat, 11–6, Sun, 2–6. See HHCG. Garden shop. On S edge of Luton on A6129. Exit 10 from M1.

Luton Hoo is a magnificent house in a magnificent setting. When Lord Bute resigned as 1st Lord of the Treasury in 1763 and retired to his recently acquired estate, he commissioned Robert Adam to remodel the house and Lancelot Brown to lay out the 1,500-acre park. By 1774 the two lakes formed from the River Lee, the cascade and the plantations were established and Brown received over £10,000 for his services. The house was altered again, by Smirke, in 1827, substantially rebuilt after a disastrous fire in 1843 and remodelled again in 1903 by Mewes and Davis, architects of the Ritz, Carlton and Waldorf hotels. The garden was also developed early in this century, providing the intimacy lacking in open parkland.

South of the house is a terraced garden. The upper terrace is private. From the middle terrace, bordered with herbaceous plants and roses, broad steps descend to the magnificent rose garden planted entirely with roses of peach, pink and soft yellow. Sculptured yew hedges create the perfect backdrop and twin pavilions provide seats, shelter and views over the upper valley of the park. Roses also fill a semi-circular apse within the enclosing hedges of the nearby tennis court.

Away from the house the path winds southwards along the upper slope of the valley, among groups of flowering trees, to the rock garden. The rocky dell, heavily screened by tall shrubs, is a world on its own. Towering rocks, dark caverns, bridges and streams create a scene of great beauty. Unfortunately, as skilled staff are especially difficult to find on the fringes of industrial Luton, the planting of the rock garden has suffered but it remains a memorable feature.

Although not intended in its day as a scenic attraction, the kitchen garden shares in the bold character of the gardens as a whole. The hexagonal brick-walled garden was built in 1906 and the range of glass still houses grapes, figs and peaches. The central conservatory range has been converted to a shop and the walled garden is a garden centre with the double advantage that it should continue to flourish and, unlike the rest of the garden, will be open all year round.

Luxmoore's, Fellows and Provost's Gardens, Eton, Berks

5 acres; 4 gardeners; clay soil. Open once in June for NGS. ½ mile N of Windsor on E side of A332 (Windsor–Slough).

The Fellows' Garden is a typical College garden. A rectangle of lawn shaded by cedars is enclosed by the College buildings on one side and by an herbaceous border on two others. The youngest cedar was a gift to the present Provost from the President of Lebanon. A wall separates the Headmaster's Garden, where the rectangular lines of a former kitchen garden are softened by curving shrub borders. A hedge screens this pleasure garden from greenhouses and cut-flower borders.

The Provost's Garden nearby is shaded by high buildings on the south and east sides and by a high wall on the west. A large *Quercus ilex* increases the shade within but plants have been chosen which thrive even against the **high** north-facing wall. Outside the railed fourth side of the square is a sunken garden built in the former stable-yard *c.*1920 to commemorate King Prajodipokh of Siam, an old Etonian.

Luxmoore's Garden is quite separate and quite different. It lies across a field from the Cloisters and its separation is emphasized by the steeply arched bridge at the entrance, with a Greek inscription on the gate bidding dogs and murderers to stay outside. The garden was created late in the nineteenth century by a College housemaster as a peaceful retreat. The central pool and sculpture are surrounded by many shrubs and trees some of which have grown to great size. The enormous *Cercis siliquastrum* is perhaps most notable. Away from the more highly developed centre an informal path through rough grass borders the Thames. The willows are cut back regularly to reveal the College spires.

Mackerye End, Harpenden, Herts

$2\frac{1}{2}$ acres plus paddocks; 2 gardeners; alkaline clay much altered by cultivation. Open once in April and June for NGS. From A6129 W of Wheathampstead, turn N at 'Cherry Tree' and follow signs to Mackerye End.

This Tudor house, concealed behind a symmetrical façade in 1665, forms an elegant picture framed by yew hedges which line the drive. Behind the yew hedge to the left is a paddock thickly carpeted with Lent Lily (*Narcissus pseudonarcissus*), reason enough for opening the garden in April. The matching hedge to the right conceals a rose garden and swimming pool around which larger shrub roses are planted.

In the forecourt is a huge *Liriodendron*, originally one of a pair planted soon after its introduction to Britain. Its young partner was planted in 1952. The other notable tree at Mackerye End is a *Ginkgo biloba*, again one of the first in the country and now overshadowing a walled courtyard west of the house. It fruited heavily for the first time in 1976. From its shade one passes into the orchard, underplanted with bulbs.

The kitchen garden, adjacent to the house, has been developed as a market garden, but not a market garden as is commonly understood. Old box hedges and espalier fruit remain along the paths but the beds are filled with unusual flowers and foliage highly prized by West End florists. Irises, single paeonies, delphiniums, alstroemerias, unusual chrysanthemums and many other flowers are grown in the garden and greenhouse.

Camellias flourish on the north side of the house near the kitchen garden and have also been planted recently, with rhododendrons, in the woodland which borders the north side of the garden, following the discovery of a patch of acid soil on this otherwise alkaline clay site. Woodland paths link the kitchen garden, the rose garden and between them wide borders of shrubs, herbaceous plants and lilies backed by the yew hedges which return along the drive, completing an attractive and varied garden.

The Manor House, Bledlow, Bucks

5 acres; 2 gardeners; fertile loam over chalk. Open once in June for NGS. 8 miles S of Aylesbury, ½ mile off B4009 in middle of Bledlow.

Although the Manor House is mainly seventeenth-century, the garden is relatively new. It was begun soon after 1945 with the planting of beech and yew hedges and pleached limes to enclose the drive and its lawn from the fields, and continued slowly thereafter. In 1966, further major changes began, creating the garden as it now is. The swimming pool and its garden replaced part of the orchard. In the following year the burning down of a barn on the south-east side of the house provided the impetus for an elegant sunken garden and in 1968 the north-west garden, the main link between house and swimming pool, was altered. Already the garden has a settled, mature appearance.

The short drive, between the kitchen garden wall and pleached limes, opens onto lawn with occasional trees. From the forecourt north-east of the house there are several openings to explore.

A newly hedged circular garden, freely planted in paving crevices and around the margins, continues as a grass walk above the elaborate sunken garden, designed by Robert Adams, and built into a steep cross slope between house and barns. A long border of old roses screens the tennis court, and a simple pattern of gravel and grass leads back to the house and drive.

Across the forecourt a path descending in shallow steps to the road connects gardens on either side. The terrace north west of the house also descends in two shallow steps, to an open lawn bounded by herbaceous borders, shrubs and trees. Roses and lavender along the terrace encourage visitors to re-cross the path into a former rose garden, now a 'knot-garden' of box-hedged compartments filled with grey- and gold-leaved plants. This colour scheme is repeated and expanded in the next enclosure, but in contrast to the trim pattern of box, the planting here is soft and flowing with herbs, roses, shrubs and herbaceous plants all contributing to a pastel garden of white, yellow and blue. Paths lead back to the cross-path or on, between swimming pool and orchard, to the croquet lawn, the kitchen garden and drive.

Manor House, Clifton Hampden, Oxon

3 acres plus 2-acre orchard; 1½ gardeners; chalk soil with steep bank to Thames. Open once each May, Sept for NGS, and each Sun in Feb for NSPCC etc. 7 miles S Oxford on A415 at E end Clifton Hampden. 4 miles E Abingdon.

The Manor House, in fact a former vicarage, has been inhabited by the same gardening family since it was built by Gilbert Scott in 1846. The steep bank of the Thames was developed in 1850–1860; John Lomax Gibbs grew the cedar which now graces the west end of the garden from seed which he brought from Lebanon in 1867. In 1903 Lord Aldenham, brother of Vicary Gibbs, moved to Clifton Hampden, bringing with him many plants from the Aldenhams' famous garden in Hertfordshire. The present owner has also enriched the garden, especially in the vegetable garden where borders relying heavily on grey foliage to support and emphasize the flowers are full of interest throughout the season.

The deeply shaded entrance and the long border down to the cedar contain many old plants but the attractive grey border in dry soil beneath the cedar is the present owner's creation. The river bank, now inaccessible in places, is rich in many varieties of snowdrop, crocus and other bulbs also planted by the present owner.

The walk above the river bank leads to the bottom of a long pergola then continues along a newly-planted laburnum walk. Beyond the walk new steps descend between banks of shrub roses to link the gardens above with the accessible part of the river bank below. A great cube of yew at the junction of house and pergola marks the entrance to the vegetable garden, the central axis of which is criss-crossed with flower borders already referred to.

The Manor House, Little Marlow, Bucks

12 acres; 3 gardeners; flinty clay soil. Open once in June, jointly for GS, NGS. S of A4155 midway between Marlow and Bourne End.

The Manor House, like many old houses, commands four quite different prospects. The entrance beneath tall limes on the east side is between the walled yard and the church. The south lawn slopes gently to a canal overhung by willows, once part of a larger formal garden. A statue of a swan on the lawn is an appropriate centrepiece. To the west a wide terrace and elegant scrollwork of box provide the foreground for an extensive lawn. A heather and birch garden designed by the owner conceals the tennis court, beyond which are shrubs and young beech for shelter in years ahead.

The main feature is north of the house. The kitchen garden has been condensed into a walled yard by the entrance allowing the original kitchen garden to be converted into an ornamental garden. The design, by Peter Coates in 1964, cleverly disguises the far from rectangular shape of the enclosure: the west end is only half the width of the east. A sunken canal divides the area, to the east of which is a circular garden of purple plum, roses, grey-leaved plants and lilacs. From its centre a vista extends across the canal to an answering 'centre' of four sculptured yews. In fact the focus is very much off-centre but the imbalance is concealed by informal shrub borders grading from conspicuous silver foliage on the right to dark purple on the left to achieve a visual balance.

The present kitchen garden includes a peach and vine house, vegetables, an orchard and the dovecote in which live the black and white nun doves creating such a delightful welcome to the garden.

The Manor House, Sutton Courtenay, Oxon

5 acres plus waterside and woodland walks; 2 gardeners; alkaline clay-loam. Open once in May for NGS. 2 miles S of Abingdon, in Sutton Courtenay almost opposite church.

When the Manor House was described in *Country Life* in 1904 and 1931, it was the home of Norah Lindsay, a talented garden designer. Mrs Lindsay created a garden 'without grandeur, but not without formality', a timeless drowsy background for an old and sleepy house, and a garden in which stray seedlings were welcomed for their charming informality. The description is still very fitting.

Rather than entering by the obvious gate near the house, it is worth following the winding path just within the boundary, shaded by tall shrubs and trees including an enormous Judas tree. At a bend, a glade frames the east front of the house and former forecourt. The main drive is now overgrown with only the handsome gate piers standing out from a young grove of beech.

The Long Garden south of the house retains its columnar yews, herbaceous borders and interesting wall plants with a patina of alpine strawberry, ivy and other semi-wildlings.

In the Persian Garden behind the wall, formality approaches its nearest to grandeur. A grape-wreathed pergola in the south corner overlooks a modern 'knot' of box and berberis. A seat within the knot faces tall hedges of beech and hornbeam leading south to the vegetable garden, west between swimming pool and orchard, and north to the house with its flagged court.

The north walk also leads to the riverside past naturalized shrubs and carpets of wild flowers. It is interesting to compare the old grass strewn with fritillaries and new grass establishing on dredgings from the ditch, and few will fail to notice the difference between adjacent sprayed and unsprayed meadows. By 1904 a bird sanctuary was established in the garden and today there is much emphasis on wildlife and wild flowers in this perfect waterside setting.

Marndhill, Ardington, Oxon

3 acres; 1 gardener; heavy loam over chalk. Open once in June for NGS. On W side of Ardington 2 miles E of Wantage, S of A417.

Marndhill is an excellent example of an older garden which seems so simple and inevitable that one must look closely to see how well the various aspects of the garden have been deployed. It has been largely replanted since 1969, adding much new interest while emphasizing rather than obscuring the earlier garden.

The entrance court north of the house is enclosed by ivies on open trellis to screen without cramping the space. Conveniently near the main access is the walled garden with trained fruits and cottage-garden flowers lining cross-walks between the vegetable plots. The greenhouse and a new swimming pool are sheltered between the south- and west-facing walls.

Along the east boundary is a wide shrub border, already flourishing to an embarrassing degree. A herb garden at the east end of the house makes an appropriate transition from vegetables to flowers and an appropriate use of this dry part of the garden. Grey borders along the south front continue from the herbs and extend to line the path out to the steps. Below the terrace, on moister soil, is an herbaceous border, then the remainder of the garden is informal lawn surrounded by old trees and shrubs. In the south-east corner, which is shaded by an old shrubbery, low lying and wet, is a green border. Here ferns, hellebores, hostas and other interesting plants provide a cool retreat and make a great asset out of a difficult situation.

Melchbourne Park, Melchbourne, Beds

10 acres in 100-acre park; clay soil. Open once or twice in June/July for NGS. 13 miles NW of Bedford. From A6 between Bedford and Rushden, turn for Knotting and Melchbourne; from A45 between Kimbolton and Higham Ferrers, turn for Dean.

From the cluster of farm buildings and houses leading to the main house, the view suddenly expands over a delightful English landscape garden with a lake, groups of trees and grassy slopes. The lake leads to a series of smaller ponds for wildfowl.

Nearer the house are many fine trees. Lawns, shrubs and roses lead from the house to the tennis court, swimming pool and the walled kitchen garden which is now used for commercial production, particularly of strawberries and pot plants.

Through the woodland, some newly planted with poplar and spruce, a network of concrete roads constructed by the R.A.F. during the war leads to more natural woodland walks.

The Mill, West Hendred, Oxon

2 acres; part-time help; deep clay over chalk. Open once in July for NGS. 3 miles E of Wantage. Turn S off A417 opposite 'The Hare'.

The Mill has a setting which could easily be spoiled if the simple peace of the long mill-house spanning its pond were disturbed by dabs of primulas or gunneras. Fortunately this part of the garden is devoted to smooth green turf but in more appropriate places there are plants in plenty, many quite unusual. Plants are allowed to seed freely but one suspects that weeding is done with great care because good colour combinations abound.

The east corner of the garden is steeply irregular with springs feeding an exciting small water garden. A hedge of shrubs leads around above the end of the house to look over mill-pond and a group of new trees.

On the west side the drive is separated from the main garden by a long border in which plants jostle thickly to maintain a long season of interest. Roses, campanulas and alstroemerias flower among the seed heads of *Baptisia australis* and the foliage of *Hemerocallis*, paeonies and carpets of *Hepatica*, handsome remnants of an earlier flowering period.

At the end of the garden, through a grove of small trees, a bridge over the stream leads to a shaded garden of hosta, primula, rodgersia and other bold plants. The shaded seclusion adds brilliance to the colour of these plants and peace to the garden beyond.

Mill House, Sutton Courtenay, Oxon

---

5 acres; 1½ gardeners; low-lying alkaline clay soil. Open twice in June for GS, NGS. 2 miles S of Abingdon. Turn S off A415 (Abingdon–Dorchester) at Culham then right at end of road. House on right.

The Mill House garden was begun in 1953. Most of it is on two islands, with backwaters of the Thames widening into a large irregular mill-pool before cascading into the mill. Although the islands are informal in character, there are many formal features creating a romantic atmosphere. Roses are used freely in the wilder areas, creating much the same impression of woodland brilliance in June as one associates with rhododendrons in May.

The garden entrance is north of the house with a small brick-paved rose garden on the right, against the house, and the ruined mill on the left. Old roses, used so well in the garden, are made double attractive by their reflection in the mill-pool. A 'Kiftsgate' rose over the bridge nearly conceals the entrance to the 'Italian Garden' within the mill. Brick paved, the garden is overshadowed by a white flowering cherry but *Acer japonicum* 'Aureum' and a reflecting mirror bring rays of light.

Across the pool a wilder character predominates. An avenue of crab apples skirts a small spring garden to reach an elegant pavilion on the river bank. Mown paths meander over the undulations of the low islands (difficult but not impossible for wheelchairs) and everywhere are signs of carefully considered plantings. Roses scramble over a huge fallen trunk with *Vitis coignetiae* for autumn brilliance. Groups of small trees – birch, *Sorbus, Metasequoia* – and shrub roses for summer and autumn interest abound. An avenue of green and golden yews begins with an arch of weeping beech and ends in a second spring garden of crab apples and cherries on the point of the second island.

The return to the house is no less interesting. A Venetian gargoyle set into the centre bridge is overhung by wisteria and pink cherry. At the point of the pool a second wisteria, white flowered, twines through a large ash. Across the bridge is a peaceful stretch of smooth lawn. Two ancient yews almost conceal the house and the garden ends with a shaded border of hellebores beneath *Hydrangea petiolaris* against the north-facing wall, given added height by pleached limes.

Milton Manor, Oxon

20 acres; 1½ gardeners; thin chalk soil. House and garden open weekends April–Oct, 2–6 (coaches by appt in week). See HHCG. In Milton by church; on B4016 4 miles S of Abingdon.

Milton Manor House stands back from the village street, behind the church. The first glimpse was tragically altered when tall elms framing the view across the lake were felled in 1975 but it is still a charming setting. Behind the house there are fine trees including a superb cut-leaved beech almost rubbing shoulders with a copper beech. In the north corner, a shaded garden with two small pools and a temple built into the garden wall leads into 'the plantation'. This long thin belt of trees with yew on the outer boundary has views back across the field to the house, an elegant seventeenth-century structure with wings added in 1762.

The one-acre walled garden north of the entrance drive conceals a very different type of garden. The southern half is now entirely ornamental: shade borders along the walls have many interesting plants while the two main panels are grassed, each with two island beds of shrubs planted by Hillier and Sons in 1968. The quartered plan is still obvious, however, with a double herbaceous border framed by rose arches and backed by fruit trees along the main axis. Beech hedges enclose panels of grass and screen the greenhouses on the south-facing wall with reduced but productive vegetable gardens on either side.

Moor Place, Much Hadham, Herts

4 acres; clay-loam soil. Open once in May/June for NGS. Midway between Bishops Stortford and Ware. Lodge gates by war memorial in centre of Much Hadham.

Moor Place is a garden of great variety, with large trees and shrubs from nineteenth-century plantings, later formal gardens and very recent developments within the old kitchen gardens.

The main house, eighteenth-century with more recent extensions, has simple surroundings – a circular forecourt enclosed by limes on the west side and open lawns with twin summerhouses (1938), pergola, pond and yew hedges on the south. The house and this south garden are encircled by a drive to the stable block, but the drive is completely hidden by a dense planting of trees and shrubs. There are many unusual shrubs, some grown to large size, one of the oldest *Davidia involucrata* in Britain, an enormous Judas Tree (*Cercis siliquastrum*) and other fine trees. The well-shaped *Liriodendron* was planted 40 years ago to replace an aged oak which looked about to collapse. The oak continues to flourish! A winding walk through the shrubs, beneath a large *Cedrela sinensis*, leads to the kitchen gardens with two one-acre walled enclosures.

One retains the old layout of four squares and a peripheral walk with some of the old fruit trees lining the paths. Two of the four squares are now grass and some paths are now lined by vigorous climbing roses and flower borders but it otherwise remains a productive kitchen garden. The second enclosure is now a garden in itself. A house in one corner was extended in 1973 and a new garden planted with curving mixed borders around the walls. A mounded area and small pool provide a focal point within the large lawn and the garden contains many unusual plants.

Between the square 'kitchen gardens' and the curved drive a small formal garden of old roses is concealed and, at some distance from the drive, a small pool with an island is being developed gradually as a wild garden.

Nether Winchendon House, Aylesbury, Bucks

4 acres; 2 gardeners; soil varies from limestone to loam to clay with periodic flooding of lower areas. Open once or twice in April, July and Aug for GS, NGS. See also HHCG. Parties by appt. May to Aug. 6 miles W of Aylesbury, 1 mile N of A418 (Aylesbury–Thame).

This Tudor manor-house, once the home of Sir Francis Bernard, Governor of Massachusetts, has a castellated screen and tower, forming a picturesque backdrop to the garden. Although old, the garden as it is seen today dates largely from 1958 when the first of many hedges was planted. (A chart showing their planting dates is on display at open days.) In 1973 the old lime avenue, then in a state of advanced decay, was felled and replaced by *Metasequoia glyptostroboides*. The hedges and avenue combine with older garden walls to create a series of gardens of considerable interest.

In the first garden, a plain rectangle of grass is flanked by a yew hedge on one side and a border on two others. Herbaceous plants and roses are combined with a varied backdrop of climbers on the walls. Taking advantage of the southerly aspect, there are also many interesting shrubs, including some well-formed *Hibiscus syriacus*.

The old kitchen garden now accommodates a tennis court and small rose garden. The latter, with thyme-planted millstones on its four sides, is bordered on three sides by young trained fruit underplanted with flowers, perpetuating a scheme widely used in older gardens. Against the east wall is a sunken and very sheltered semi-circular garden with many tender plants. The nearby potting shed, adapted from a nineteenth-century greenhouse and still containing the old door fittings, staging etc., should not be overlooked.

Beyond the wall is the present kitchen garden where old doorways add interest and paths, some of mediaeval origin, lead into the woodland which was once part of a much larger garden. Below the vegetable garden is the arboretum with many young trees and a sound policy of thinning to ensure that the best of them can grow into good specimens. From here one emerges onto open lawn extending from the house to the river below. Across the lawn is the main shrubbery balancing the arboretum and enclosing a wide curving walk up again to the house.

Nettlebed Gardens, Oxon

Several gardens in historical brick-making village. Clay-loam merging into clay with flints and shallow soil over chalk on slopes. Open once in June/July for NGS. At E end of Nettlebed (midway between Henley-on-Thames and Wallingford on A423) turn N for Crocker End.

The gardens include:

Little Hill (⅔ acre; no gardener): Little Hill was built in 1935 and the small roughly triangular garden on the edge of the woods developed gradually from 1952 to 1973. It is now maintained as a memorial to its creator by her husband.

A wide rose border lines the main path. The rest of the garden is of grass and mixed borders, difficult to describe in a small space but pleasant to explore. Much thought is evident in choosing plants to suit the varied conditions around the house. To the south is a silver pear on a lawn fringed by rowan and beech woods. In the south-west corner are more tender shrubs lining a small path to a second, minor entrance and partially concealing the vegetable plot. Here the garden is particularly full, varied and interesting.

The east and north sides are more open. Shrub roses and a curving herbaceous border bound the main lawn, leading to a sunken circular lawn by a willow. Azaleas and heathers are planted above a small orchard and, against the house itself, is a damp, shaded bed of *Hosta*, *Cornus* and similar plants.

The Malt House (1 acre; no gardener): The picturesque house and barn with a paved court between, in themselves attractive enough to justify a visit, occupy about half the garden. West of the house is a small lawn with rose beds and an old apple tree adding to the bright cottage garden appearance. Against the west-facing wall of a triangular walled garden is a mounded rock garden with a pool and small waterfall.

Waterpits (¾ acre; one gardener): Waterpits was made from two seventeenth-century cottages in 1972. The semi-circular drive east of the house is separated from the garden by a shrub border, but most of the remainder of the garden is open to exploit the view. In the eastern corner is a vegetable garden. Borders of roses and hydrangeas lead to the main lawn and terrace west of the house, and much of the garden, the terrace in particular, is bright with annuals. Two low herbaceous borders as a foreground for the view across the field with the old waterpit which gave the house its name, and into the valley beyond. Finally, in the south-west corner, is a small cut-flower garden secluded from the rest of the garden by old and new hedges.

North Mymms Park, North Mymms, Herts

12 acres in large park; 2 gardeners with help in spring-cleaning from 5 market garden staff. Open once each for NGS, RC in June/July. W of A1 between Hatfield (5 miles) and South Mimms (2 miles).

North Mymms House was built in 1593 and much extended in the nineteenth century. Although much simplified, the garden retains much of its grandeur and many interesting plants. The large wing added to the house in 1893 was removed in 1945, leaving only the loggia, but William Robinson's design for the garden has fared better.

The drive arrives at the west front, overlooking wide grass terraces. Yew hedges flanking the house reveal, on the south side, the magnificent paved rose garden. Each of the many beds is filled with one cultivar of hybrid tea rose and edged with pinks etc. spilling onto the wide paths. The east wall with its sheltered alcove remains from the Victorian wing.

Below the rose garden is a walled garden, once lined with herbaceous borders but now planted with floribunda roses. In the shrub garden to the east, many of the shrubs have grown to great size and these, too, have been interplanted with roses, including 'Mrs Walter Burns' named after the owner. The 'Italian Garden', on the upper level of the same high-walled enclosure, also remains. The main cross-walk of the lofty pergola encloses four compartments each subdivided into four smaller squares with a magnolia or other shrub. As in other parts of the garden, many large climbers remain, including here *Hydrangea petiolaris* and *Actinidia kolomikta*, while urns and statues terminate the shaded vistas.

Across the drive from the old kitchen gardens, now a commercial market-garden, the extensive area of grass, flowering trees and yew hedges remain from a once elaborate pleasure ground while nearer the house are more formal enclosures.

In the courtyard the loggia already mentioned is the coolest place in the garden on a hot day. To the north is a second court enclosed by the

5 Savill Garden, Windsor Great Park: water, waterside reflections and waterside plants create many beautiful pictures in this superb woodland garden

6 Wrest Park: the scrolls of gravel, turf and box in the parterre, of which only half is shown here, are seen best from the air. The canal and Archer's pavilion, barely discernible in the distance, extend the grandeur of the garden into the countryside

7 White Cottage: the small rose garden, enclosed by box hedge, has been enriched with a wide variety of cushion and trailing plants to provide interest throughout the year. Outside the hedge there are bearded iris and an excellent small mixed border

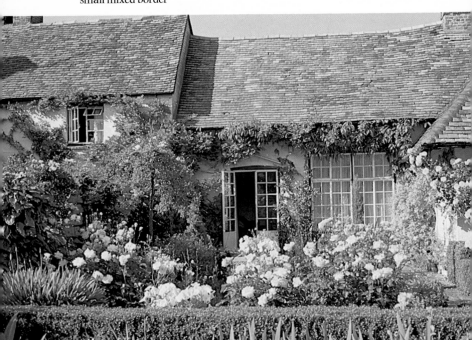

house and two gazebos. This court is reminiscent of Hatfield or Montacute not only in appearance but in having once served as the main approach to the house (*c.*1820 to 1893). Along the unaltered north front is a balustraded terrace overlooking an expanse of grass and cedars out to the curved ha-ha. An opening in the yew hedge returns again to the west drive.

Nuneham, Nuneham Courtenay, Oxon (University of Oxford)

27 acres; 1 gardener with help from estate; clay soil. Open 2—5.30 on Aug Bank Hol weekend and immediately preceding and following weekend. See HHCG. 4 miles S of Oxford. 1 mile W of A423 (Oxford–Maidenhead) along drive from middle of village.

Few places can be as important as Nuneham in the history of gardening. The Palladian villa was begun by the 1st Earl Harcourt in 1756 on a knoll overlooking the Thames, a site chosen for its natural beauty. From 1760 the Earl proceeded to pull down the old village and replace the mediaeval church by a domed temple. A grass terrace extended northwards to recreate classical scenes with the spires of Oxford as a noble substitute for Rome itself.

The 2nd Earl, an artist and egalitarian, sought a less ostentatious setting. Immediately upon his succession in 1777 he commissioned Lancelot Brown to open the oak forest to the south and to alter the house. The result, a sublime English landscape, was one of Brown's last and best works.

Even before his succession, the 2nd Earl employed the poet William Mason to design a concealed flower garden, expressing Rousseau's philosophy that Nature, grand in her large designs, was greater still in her smallest works. Climbers festooned from trees and arched over rustic bowers 'weaving a garland of repose' while urns and weeping trees created a pleasing melancholy which deepened in the gloom of the grotto. Despite the strong disapproval of the old Earl, it is the only poet's garden still surviving.

Mason also reshaped the vistas from the north terrace in accordance with the picturesque principles of William Gilpin, whose nephew,

William Sawrey Gilpin, planted the Scots pines which still divide the panoramic view from the house into a series of picturesque scenes. Young Gilpin also re-introduced the balustraded terrace and replanted Mason's garden. On the lower hillside the 1st Viscount Harcourt added a wild garden in 1904, inspired by his friend William Robinson and this garden, too, remains in part.

In 1948 Oxford University purchased the estate and from 1969 Culham College of Education partially restored the terraces and Mason's garden. With a new tenancy negotiated in 1977, the prospect for the future may be brighter still, although sensitive treatment will be essential. A garden created by poets, philosophers and artists could as easily be destroyed as saved by misguided zeal.

Oakfield, Mortimer, Berks

4-acre garden plus 8-acre lake and woodlands; 1 gardener; gravel soil. Open once in May for NGS. 5 miles SW of Reading and 1 mile E Burghfield Common. From A33 at Three Mile Cross turn W for Grazeley Green and Wokefield.

The early eighteenth-century house is set in oak woodlands which create ideal conditions for the rhododendrons and camellias along the drive. Sequoiadendron, cedar and other large trees indicate the garden's nineteenth-century character but it has been rescued from prolonged neglect and much added to since 1950.

Cornus for winter interest, azaleas, cherries and bulbs for spring, and roses for summer have been planted in large groups around the open lawn west of the house. The poor gravelly soil suits many trees with good autumn colour and their grouping west of the house is doubly advantageous, giving illumination by the setting sun and reflection in the lake which forms such an important feature of the garden.

The lake brings light and distant prospect to an otherwise heavily wooded area. Also, its supporting dam with the overflow stream at its foot is being developed as an exciting wooded dell in which rhododendrons, magnolias, camellias, embothriums and other interesting plants flourish.

A path through the dell returns to an old partially walled garden, now planted with roses. At the south end are flowering trees in grass.

To the north an enormous *Cercis siliquastrum* and *Quercus ilex* overhang a small orchid house.

The garden as a whole merges easily into the surrounding woodland through which longer walks have been cut.

Odell Castle, Odell, Beds

---

6 acres; $1\frac{1}{2}$ gardeners; stony soil overlying clay. Open once in June and July for NGS. 9 miles NW of Bedford between A6 and A428.

Odell Castle was built in 1962 using the stone and original site of the Georgian and Victorian 'castle' which burned in the 1930s. The old terrace has been retained with fine views across the River Ouse which forms one boundary.

The main garden is open grass with tall beech, horse chestnuts and pink chestnut reinforced by new plantings of shade trees, flowering cherries and fruit to echo the curved lines of the main descent from the terrace.

East of the house is a large vegetable garden. To the west, within the outlines of an older vegetable garden, are new trees, many received as gifts. Catalpa, ginkgo, koelreuteria and cedars are among the new plantings. This level is separated from the main lawn by beds of floribunda roses, with vigorous shrub roses and an herbaceous border framing a walk to the west steps of the terrace. The terrace wall itself supports tender wall shrubs and, on the house itself, 'Albertine' rose and a wisteria are rapidly colonizing the south façade from opposite corners.

Odney Club, Cookham, Berks

120 acres; 7 gardeners; neutral gravel and sand over chalk. Open once in May for NGS. On E side of A4094 (Maidenhead–Bourne End) just S of Cookham Bridge.

Below Cookham Bridge the Thames divides into four channels with several minor streams. The gardens of Odney Club include two islands in their 120 acres and the river adds much interest to the flat garden, as do the fine trees growing in the well-drained but well-watered alluvial soil.

The gardens have been developed from older gardens acquired with the several houses added to the club since it began in 1927. The yew-hedged rose garden and herbaceous borders were early additions and more recently several borders have been replanted with shrubs which are easy to grow, easy to propagate and mainly evergreen: excellent models for those trying to establish a new garden. New and old are intermingled, however. The rose garden was designed around a large blue cedar and, in the new Management Training Centre, eucalyptus and other tender shrubs planted in 1973 share the sheltered walled garden with a fine old weeping beech.

Apart from tennis courts and a new swimming pool the main island is open grass, made even more open by the loss of many large elms, but there is much to see beyond. The smaller Formosa Island has some fine eighteenth-century cedars on the north end, enormous planes over-hanging the river on the south, and views across the river to the steep slopes of Cliveden. A backwater between the two islands has been developed intermittently as a water garden. In recent years much progress has been made despite problems of fluctuating water levels and, as often happens in larger waterside gardens, interest is supplemented by wild flowers, birds and other wildlife.

The Old Crown, Long Crendon, Bucks

1 acre; part-time gardener; sandy loam over limestone. Open once in June for NGS. 2 miles N of Thame, on B4011 (Thame–Bicester) at lower end of Long Crendon village.

This long, relatively narrow garden slopes down steeply to the south west and has, as a result, many sheltered corners as well as fine views. It has been restored since 1970 and, although it is opened mainly for roses, there are many other plants of interest.

The forecourt opens into the upper garden, with a border of herbaceous plants and annuals against the upper boundary wall. There is a smaller annual border against the greenhouse with a herb border and central asparagus bed providing a green foil and welcome food. At the lower edge of this level, a small but effective border of blue, green and white marks the steps down to the next terrace. This is planted with HT roses and looks down through a vista of climbing roses between the vegetables and orchard on one side and informal shrubs on the other. Its terminus is provided by a border of shrub and species roses backed by a young 'Kiftsgate' rose.

In the south corner the lowest point is marked by a spring-fed pool shaded by sycamores, ash and willows in contrast to the sunny slope. Grass paths wind up among the shrubs to a long flight of steps around a rock garden and back to the forecourt. However, one should not overlook the small, very sheltered, steeply terraced garden behind the house where wisteria, ceanothus and *Akebia quinata* thrive.

Old Farm, Bishopstone, Bucks

1½ acres; 1 gardener; clay soil. Open once each June, July for GS, NGS. 4 miles SW Aylesbury; from A418 Thame–Aylesbury, at Stone church turn S for Bishopstone; Old Farm at S end of village.

This garden was started in 1948 and demonstrates admirably what can be achieved in a long narrow plot. The boundaries are thickly planted, as are the margins of the natural pool at the end of the garden, thus enclosing a long winding walk around the pool. Glimpses of the pool, patches of light and shade and the plants themselves offer much of interest, especially to photographers. Beyond the pool is a quite separate vegetable garden and tucked against one boundary is a small rose garden, formal and secluded.

Small island beds with winding grass paths make a gradual transition from the dense planting of the main part of the garden to the open lawn around the house, the boundary planting continuing with brighter flowers of annuals and herbaceous perennials at the edge of the lawn and along the gravel drive.

A wall dividing the flower garden from the yard shelters a paved sitting area richly planted in crevices, on walls and in surrounding borders, but it does not mark the end of the garden. A gateway in the wall leads across the yard to a small group of old fruit trees now garlanded with clematis and screened from the road by willows and coloured-stemmed dogwoods.

The Old House, North Dean, Bucks

1 acre; no gardener; shallow soil over chalk. Open Apr–Oct by appt. only for NGS. 4 miles N of High Wycombe. From A4128 (to Hughenden and Great Missenden) take road to Speen.

The Old House and its stables, now a showroom for antiques, are at one end of this irregularly shaped garden, dividing it into several smaller units each planted for a limited season of effect. The drive is separated from the main lawn by borders of late-flowering herbaceous plants and roses, supplemented with begonias and other tender perennials. Roses also feature in a sunken garden against the yew hedge which screens the recently abandoned vegetable garden. A new vegetable garden, in a beech-hedged enclosure above the lawn, creates a more compact and manageable unit.

Between the house and showroom, a brick courtyard meanders through softening planting to the pointed lower end of the garden. Even this small area is subdivided: flanking borders of winter-flowering plants extend forward to separate a small lily pond and lawn from a miniature glade beyond. On the upper side of the house the path is edged by a low retaining wall planted with spring flowers, and emerges between conifers and shrub roses to the main lawn which gains in apparent extent by its contrast with the tiny spring garden.

The Old House, Wheatley, Oxon

$1\frac{1}{2}$ acres plus $2\frac{1}{2}$-acre paddock and pond; no gardener; clay soil. Open once in April and July for NGS. 5 miles E of Oxford, turn S off A40 to Wheatley then into Kiln Lane, at low point in Church Road.

The Old House is half concealed from the entrance court by jasmine, honeysuckle, ceanothus and pyracantha. Roses, though, are the main feature of the garden. An old apple tree supports 'Wedding Day' and *Rosa longicuspis* while the tender *R.odorata* climbs on a sheltered wall across the lawn.

There are more roses across the stream which divides the open lawn from the orchard planted with bulbs. The stream itself is not much developed as water rats eat any new plants, but a gravel path through the shrubbery alongside the stream terminates at a new, informal rose garden, well labelled and well planted with all types of roses. A vigorous rose hedge conceals the vegetable plot. A second path bordered by espalier fruit leads between the vegetable garden and orchard to a large pond with several interesting breeds of duck. Finally, a curving path returns through the orchard, past a small shade garden thickly planted with hostas, euphorbias, hellebores and other such plants to the entrance court.

The Old Parsonage, Buscot, Oxon (The National Trust)

1 acre; no gardener; heavy alkaline loam. Open Wed, 2–6 by appt. with the tenant. See HHCG. N of A417 between Lechlade (1½ miles) and Faringdon (4½ miles).

This is an interesting house and the garden is no less so.

Developed mainly since 1965 within the walls of an older garden, it consists of a series of enclosures of varied size and character. There are young camellias in the small sheltered patio between the house and its surrounding wall but the rest of the garden is restricted to lime-tolerant plants. Despite occasional flooding of the Thames which borders the garden and more frequent inundation by water from the corners of the roof, many grey-leaved plants are included in the informal association of shrubs, herbaceous plants and numerous spring and autumn bulbs, combining with the Cotswold stone walls to give a soft, light effect.

South of the house is a small lavender-hedged garden connected through a tunnel of yew to the main garden. The borders around the main lawn abound in good plant combinations, and the old apple in the centre supports *Clematis montana*.

A gate in the north wall leads to the kitchen garden. From the kitchen garden one can go through a gate in the low wall to a small riverside garden or in the higher east wall to the yard, where a circle of eight apple trees is being engulfed by a 'Kiftsgate' rose. The barn which separates the yard and riverside has been converted into a studio/garden room with a raised indoor swimming pool, an ideal combination of building and garden.

The Old Rectory, Bletsoe, Beds

$4\frac{1}{2}$ acres; no gardener; clay soil. Open once in June for NGS. 7 miles N of Bedford, turn E off A6 at 'Falcon Arms'. House opposite church.

The Old Rectory garden is largely Victorian but has been greatly simplified.

The south front, clothed in a grape vine which has long outlived its conservatory, looks over the old circular drive to a shady group of trees including a fine cut-leaved beech and weeping pink hawthorn. A new small vegetable garden lies beyond. From the west front of the house gravel paths, still tile edged, wind to left, between shrubberies, and to right between herbaceous borders to a small rose garden. Near the house are tall evergreens: a redwood, yews and a cedar which, because its branches have been propped up, has spread until it almost conceals the house.

The Old Rectory, Burghfield, Berks

$4\frac{1}{2}$ acres plus 14-acre park; 1 gardener; clay soil but much modified. Open last Wed, Mar–Oct inclusive except Aug for GS, NGS, RC etc; plant sales. $5\frac{1}{2}$ miles SW of Reading. Turn S off A4 W of Reading to Burghfield; turn right after Hatch Gate Inn; entrance on right.

The Old Rectory garden is convincing proof that good design and a love of plants are not mutually exclusive. Bulbs and new trees in the paddock bordering the drive are the first indications of horticultural interest. Across the lawn from the main garden-side of the house, twin yew hedges planted in 1959 back herbaceous borders then turn at right-angles, framing a vista to the Roman statue in an informal pond beyond.

Against the south-west facing wall the lawn is edged by a deep curving border with many good plants, from a large, fruitful *Callicarpa bodinieri* near the house to a mound of *Solanum jasminoides*. The solanum conceals a small greenhouse filled with orchids and other interesting plants. The adjacent small paved area, the floor of a former second greenhouse, has plants in and on the walls, in the floor, in pots and borders. Perhaps the most beautiful is *Geranium palmatum* (*G.maderiense*), its dissected leaves up to ten inches across.

To the right of the hedges, beyond a cedar, is a croquet lawn fringed by lavender hedges and a tennis court concealed by azaleas, Japanese maples and other beautiful plants. To the left, an opening in the 'L' shaped yew hedge reveals an attractive swimming pool and a shrub rose border, supplemented with many tender plants. Beyond this is another square garden but the planting here is completely informal: the square is not separated from the rest of the wild garden stretching to the end of the garden and around the informal pool to new borders near the tennis court. Small maples shade a profusion of hellebores, violas, primulas and many delightful woodland plants and bulbs.

The back yard, too, is interesting, with its alcove of sink gardens and, along the brick path leading to the old (1580) part of the house, a narrow green border with spurges, green primroses, plantains and so on. Across the vegetable garden a collection of old varieties of fruit trees is being established with a garden of old roses.

The great interest of the garden is remarkable when one considers that the owner had no interest in gardening until 1956 and that she has planted all except the obviously pre-1950 plants. Since 1960 the Old Rectory has formed a focus for keen plantsmen because there is a 'mini-market' at each open day with stalls set up by specialists to distribute unusual plants and enthusiasm.

The Old Rectory, Farnborough, Berks

---

4 acres; 1 gardener; thin chalk soil but heavily manured. Open once in June for NGS. 4 miles SE of Wantage. From B4494 (Wantage–Newbury) turn E at signpost for Farnborough.

The Old Rectory combines a simple setting of beech, grass and bulbs at the approach to the elegant house with richly planted gardens at the back. Clematis are well represented though the garden has a wealth of other plants.

The yew hedge bordering the drive conceals wide double herbaceous borders which have been extensively replanted. Groups of beech frame a magnificent view over a ha-ha as this is probably the highest garden in Berkshire. At the side of the house, by the 1955 extension, a pool garden has clematis grown on a frame to create a 'flower-bed'. In the adjacent walled yard, a golden hop sprawls in a great sheet of yellow, while twin laburnums flank the opening which leads to the luxuriant old rose garden. Begun in 1968, this double border is underplanted with a great variety of cushion and trailing plants from silvery artemisias to the almost black-leaved *Ophiopogon planiscapus* 'Nigrescens'.

Between the walls of the yard, clothed with *Clematis tangutica*, *C.balearica* and hellebores, and the rose garden, a path leads in one direction to a beech wood and in the other direction to the 'orchard', and vegetable garden. Two old apple trees of the original orchard now support *Rosa longicuspis* and *R.filipes* 'Kiftsgate' while the small rectangle of grass also accommodates a mulberry, *Ginkgo, Liriodendron*, magnolias and other plants, becoming more crowded with each planting season.

Next to the orchard is a tennis court screened by *Rosa* 'Nevada' and Lawson's Cypress. Beyond this is the swimming pool, its cream-washed walls forming an ideal background for the rich purple and crimson border outside. Inside, in complete contrast, the plants are grey leaved with white or pale yellow flowers which, with the almost Indian character of the pavilion, gives a dream-like quality. Planted in 1972, the borders within the walls were so lavishly prepared with horse manure and topsoil that many plants fill their allotted space within two years.

From the pool garden one can wander through the stable-yard or the surrounding trees to the billowy shapes of tall variegated sycamores which form such a feature on arrival.

Old Rectory, Swerford, Oxon

1 acre; part-time help with vegetables; heavy loam over limestone. Open once in May for NGS. 5 miles NE of Chipping Norton. Midway between Banbury and Chipping Norton, turn N off A361 for Swerford.

The Old Rectory garden is simple in outline but varied and interesting in its planting. The house, outbuildings and garden walls are all of mellow limestone and a vista extends through house and garden to the hill beyond.

In front of the house crimson flowers and purple foliage are set off by the stone walls. The back garden is approached through a side door which opens by a flourishing *Solanum crispum,* setting the tone for a border of tender plants (*Hebe hulkeana,* Lemon Verbena, *Dictamnus,* etc.) against the south-facing wall of the house. The lawn, edged with lavender and rose 'Iceberg' leads to the main vista, a grass walk lined with shrubs grown for their foliage. Here are purple cotinus and *Prunus* 'Cistena', golden elder and elm, and the bright spring foliage of *Acer pseudoplatanus* 'Brilliantissimum' grown here as a neatly rounded shrub.

A small lateral rose-walk at the end of the hitherto concealed vegetable garden diverts the eye from the stone pillars marking the end of the garden and leads to a much narrower path between vegetables and old box hedge to the last part of the garden, a sheltered sunken garden with *Hoheria sextylosa,* campsis and other tender plants against high south- and west-facing walls. This corner is watched over by a huge wild cherry which, with a small flight of steps, separates the garden from the main lawn.

Old Rectory Cottage, Tidmarsh, Berks

1 acre; no gardener; chalk soil but low-lying and much modified. Open by appt. Apr–Oct inclusive for NGS etc; plant sales. $\frac{1}{2}$ mile S of Pangbourne. Halfway between Pangbourne and Tidmarsh turn into narrow lane immediately S of 'Old Rectory' and left at bottom.

This is the garden of a widely travelled plant collector and, as one might imagine, it consists of winding narrow paths through a fascinating collection of rare and interesting plants. The native soil is chalk but the garden is low and subject to flooding. Also, large quantities of composted sawdust and manure have been available to make raised beds edged with logs, an ideal home for the woodland plants which grow so freely. The garden started in 1958 and, after two years of clearing debris, planting began in 1960, using pigs and potato crops to break the ground. It is still expanding gradually as odd patches of potato here and there indicate.

Two sides of the house look onto comparatively open garden with island beds against a well-established coloured foliage border. A curving path between two beech hedges leads to the old orchard where apple trees each carry two or three climbers. As the ground falls towards the River Pang there is a small lake. Here willows come into prominence and other trees with attractive bark offer the light shade necessary for woodland plants. Willows are one speciality; rose species, lilies, helle-bores, bulbs in general and woodland plants are others, many plants having been brought back from the owner's travels.

This is a remarkably large garden for one man, even in active retire-ment, but there is, in addition to the main garden, an alpine house and frame used to raise many seeds and cuttings for plant sales.

The Old Vicarage, Bucklebury, Berks

---

4 acres; 1 gardener (plus help with lawns); deep alkaline clay-loam over chalk. Open once in April and June for NGS. $2\frac{1}{2}$ miles N of A4 between Reading and Newbury. 4 miles W of Exit 12 from M4. Adjoins Bucklebury church.

Although the garden is flat and sufficiently low-lying to cause late frost problems, it has attractive views along the Pang valley, views well exploited when Lanning Roper redesigned the garden in 1960. He was asked to create a spacious garden as a setting for several fine pieces of modern sculpture, and in this he succeeded admirably.

From the south a short drive curves through deep shade to the house, which faces a Henry Moore figure on a small lawn. Across the drive the trees shading the entrance also back a spring border and con-ceal the former tennis court. In 1970 this was planted with small flowering trees, with new fruit on the east side and colourful island borders around a pond at the south end.

The variety and intimacy of this corner does not impinge on the main vista forming the central third of the garden. A group of large yews in brick paving conceal the borders and, with balancing groups of yew, cherry and crab apple, frame the view to another Henry Moore figure silhouetted against the sky. A long barn and shrub rose border provide a more solid screen from the garden north of the vista. The shrub roses have taller shrubs behind and an edging of lower semi-shrubby and herbaceous plants to extend the season. Like most other parts of the garden, there is one main season of interest but the border is by no means unattractive at other times.

Vegetables, fruit, glass and playlawn occupy most of the northern third of the garden, with espalier fruit along the wide grass paths. Following the recent construction of a swimming pool, however, there is more wall space to extend still further the wide range of climbers which also furnish the house, barn, carport and their connecting walls. In the three glasshouses there is a fine collection of orchids, with cut flowers, pot plants etc. in any remaining space and in frames. South of the glasshouses, a small formal herb garden decorates the courtyard, from which arches and doors lead beneath festoons of climbers back to the vegetable garden or to the central vista.

Oxford Botanic Gardens (University of Oxford)

The Botanic Gardens are on three sites, the old Botanic Garden, the Genetic Garden and Nuneham Arboretum.

The Genetic Garden, less than an acre in extent, exists to demonstrate certain botanical principles and processes: polyploid series in cultivated plants, breeding systems, variegation and its inheritance and botanical abnormalities such as sports, fasciation, contortion and chimaeras. The garden is north of the Observatory and is open during university working hours. The *Botanic Garden* and *Nuneham Arboretum* are described below.

The Botanic Garden, High Street, Oxford

> $7\frac{1}{2}$ acres; 11 gardeners (including 3 under glass and one for seed list); alkaline soil subject to flooding in parts. Open every day except Good Friday and Christmas; weekdays 8.30–5; Suns, 10–12 and 2–6. Closes 4.30 in winter. Glasshouses open 2–4 only. S side of High Street near Magdalen Bridge.

Oxford Botanic Garden is the oldest in Britain, founded by the Earl of Danby in 1621. For 4 years the soil was manured to improve it and raise it above the Cherwell and by 1632 the 3½-acre central garden enclosed by 500 yards of wall took on a form hardly altered today. After unsuccessful attempts to obtain John Tradescant as Keeper, the post was offered in 1642 to Jacob Bobart, a neighbouring innkeeper! Bobart combined innkeeping and gardening and his son showed the same resourcefulness, selling fruit in Oxford and seeds in London to further the work of the garden. Two ancient yews remain in the garden from the avenue planted by Bobart, who is also famed as the raiser of the now ubiquitous London Plane. The garden has made many other contributions to botany.

Its plan is simple. Cross-paths quarter the main garden and the four smaller squares are largely filled with family beds of herbaceous plants and shrubs. Otherwise the planting of the garden is opportunistic. The walls themselves provide a variety of aspects for 300 different climbing plants, with tender shrubs against the south-west facing wall of the Old Botany School. Ferns, lilies and ivies are planted in north-facing borders and new trees are planted wherever space permits between older specimens. The largest American Persimmon, *Diospyros virginiana*, in Britain is in the garden and there are large trees of *Fraxinus ornus*, *Ginkgo biloba*, *Gymnocladus dioicus* and *Sorbus domestica* among others.

South of the walled garden is a rock garden, a border of historic roses, and further informal shrub collections; to the east are glasshouses, rebuilt in 1970 on much older foundations. Special collections of plants include *Berberis*, *Crocus*, *Rosa*, variegated plants, carnivorous plants and tropical plants of economic importance, but the gardens are well endowed with a wide collection of plants of all types.

The atmosphere of the garden is peaceful. It seems a world apart from the busy High Street and is an ideal haven in which to escape, eat a picnic lunch and learn about plants.

Nuneham Arboretum, Nuneham Courtenay, Oxon

50 acres; 3 gardeners (including one trainee); acid lower greensand over alkaline clay. Open weekdays 9–5. 4½ miles S of Oxford at S end of Nuneham Courtenay village, W of A423 (Oxford–Henley-on-Thames).

The 8-acre pinetum established by the Archbishop of York, Edward Harcourt, from 1830 to 1844 and enlarged by his nephew from 1855 to 1865 forms the nucleus of the Arboretum. The whole estate was purchased by the University in 1949 and 4½ acres of the original pinetum came eventually to the Botanic Garden. Because the collection included some of the first and finest examples of many conifers planted in this country, the plantation was enlarged to 50 acres in 1968 and established as a University Arboretum. The lower greensand which outcrops below the clay cap of Windmill Hill is rare in Oxfordshire and allows the cultivation of many plants which cannot be grown well in the older Botanic Garden.

The Arboretum may be divided into four main areas. The south side, extending towards the centre, has experimental plantations of several coniferous species; the western boundary, rising to Windmill Hill, has oak and mixed woodland rich in native plants and is maintained as a conservation area; to the north is open grassland in which groups of *Sorbus, Crataegus*, willow and other young trees are being established and to the east, bordering the road, is 'The Ride'.

The Ride is thought to have been laid out by William Gilpin. Although only about 5 acres have been developed it seems much more as the drive winds tortuously between banks of rhododendrons which conceal the surroundings, opening here and there to reveal new plantings. Camellias, heathers and tender Chilean shrubs such as *Embothrium* are becoming established among tall conifers including picturesque (or grotesque) *Araucaria*. Trilliums, lilies and other woodland plants grow well beneath the shrubs and add considerable interest. On the east boundary is a glade of maples, especially beautiful in their autumn colour.

Phillips Hill, Snelsmore Common, Berks

$2\frac{1}{2}$-acre garden in 60 acres of woodland; 1 gardener; gravel over clay. Open once in May for NGS. 3 miles N of Newbury on B4494 just S of M4 motorway.

Phillips Hill is opened mainly for the bluebells which carpet the oak woodland, with added interest from the fact that this is the site of a Briton hill-fort. The drive crosses the high double ridge of earthworks.

In addition to this natural and historical interest there is an attractive formal garden contemporary with the late Edwardian house. South of the house is a square rose garden with a long lily pool and surrounding of trim yew hedges. The cross axis of the rose garden leads eastwards across open lawn to a small bridge over the earthworks, here planted with rhododendrons. To the west, pollarded limes shade a narrow garden between the yew hedge and kitchen-garden wall.

The kitchen garden includes a tennis court, herb border, fruit cage, small greenhouse and frames. Vegetables are grown in large beds cut out of the turf so the area of cultivation can be increased or decreased at will, returning any ground not required to a grass ley, thus enriching the poor gravelly soil.

All the gardens have openings to the south boundary, from which fine views are obtained.

North of the house a walled forecourt faces a short lime avenue. The carpet of bluebells, daffodils, bugle and primroses beneath the limes unites the formality of the garden with its backdrop of woodland in a most delightful way.

The Priory, Beech Hill, Berks

4 acres; 1 gardener; clay-loam. Open once in June for NGS. 8 miles S of Reading. From A33 turn W opposite Spencer's Wood P.O. then sharp left at Beech Hill crossroads.

This former Benedictine priory was given by Henry VI to Eton College as part of its foundation. The present building is largely fifteenth-century, altered in the seventeenth century. Although the form of the garden was determined in the seventeenth century most of the planting is post-1945. Sited on a south-east facing slope overlooking flat farm-land and woodland, its peaceful atmosphere is emphasized by the stream, a man-made loop of the River Loddon, which marks the transition from the rectangular layout on one side to the informal garden beyond.

Below the gravel forecourt an open lawn, with the stream along its lower margin, leads into the kitchen garden. Here, narrow paths run between flower borders backed by espalier apple trees into the orchard. The large rectangles enclosed by these borders, and a large field behind the house, are devoted to market gardening.

Across the stream the 'island' has a stew-pond, enlarged before World War I, with the older part shaded by ash and a handsome oak.

The gunnera at the point of the island is especially dramatic when afternoon light shines through its giant leaves above the bold foliage of the native butterburr.

Interesting plants include the handsome young Tulip Tree, *Liriodendron tulipifera* by the stream (planted by the present owner and already flowering well), the Banksian rose and campsis in the back yard, and the rare Chinese lilac, *Syringa sweginzowii* near the dovecote. The hardy fan palm strikes a bold note in the streamside border while further along the stream the large copper beech is put to practical use as a concert platform providing acoustics usually lacking in outdoor recitals!

Purley Hall, Pangbourne, Berks

8 acres; 1 gardener; alluvial soil over plateau gravel, varying from light soil on hill to heavy in the valley. Open once in May for NGS. 1 mile E of Pangbourne S of A329 (Pangbourne–Reading).

This seventeenth-century house was altered early in the eighteenth century and in 1721 Charles Bridgeman was paid £112 11s 0d for his garden plan. Major expansions envisaged for the house were not implemented, but the garden plan was. The main element of Bridgeman's scheme, a 'Y' shaped canal west of the house, still exists in part. although the stem of the 'Y' was destroyed in 1818. The knobbly flint shelter which terminates the vista was built to commemorate the Battle of Culloden in 1745. The walled garden south of the main vista is also from the original scheme as is the huge lime east of the house but other large trees have been lost in the gales of recent years.

The rest of the garden is more recent. East of the walled garden is a Victorian grove of redwoods and other tall trees beneath which primroses, cowslips and bulbs flourish in the long grass. The border against the wall is filled largely with June flowers. The swimming pool in its own steep-sided little valley is surrounded by roses, tree paeonies and shrubs in grass.

East of the house, itself supporting magnolias, wisteria and clematis in profusion, is a sunken rose garden, above which is a raised grass walk, cleared and made in 1975. From here one can see both the garden and the surrounding farmland and woodland. On Bridgeman's plan, the woodland is shown with formal rides and garden buildings to carry the eye into the landscape, and the new walk does much to recapture this link between garden and landscape.

Pusey House, Faringdon, Oxon

15 acres; 3 gardeners; limestone soil. Open April–July, Wed, Thurs and Suns. July–mid Oct, daily except Mons and Fris. All Bank Hols. 2–6. See HHCG. Plant sales. 12 miles W of Oxford; 5 miles E of Faringdon, ½ mile S of A420.

Pusey House Garden is of two ages. The house, lake and many fine trees are eighteenth-century. The present owners came in 1935 and since the war they have planted many new trees, shrubs and herbaceous plants to enliven the garden and reduce its scale: enliven but not clutter. From the terrace (one of Geoffrey Jellicoe's first commissions, in 1937) there is no fussy planting to interrupt the sweep of lawn down to the lake, up again to the ha-ha and beyond to the hills. Sensibly the smaller plants are kept against the walls (from which they derive much warmth) and within old tree groups flanking the vistas so spaciousness and intimacy co-exist in a harmony found in few other gardens.

The central openness also facilitates a circular tour, albeit with some deviations. A printed guide gives a clear plan of the garden and extensive lists of plants in each area, so it is not necessary to dwell here on the many plants to be found, even if it were possible to do so adequately. Suffice it to say that with south-facing walls and free-draining soils sloping down to a boggy waterside, the range of plants grown is remarkable.

In 1975 a new visitors' entrance was made. Wrought iron gates lead to a double border with deep reds predominating near the entrance, fading to pastels and grey foliage. This new garden emerges near the upper end of a long curved herbaceous border against the outer wall of the kitchen garden with the house and terrace to the left and a small temple in the shady distance on the right. The paved terrace and south-facing retaining wall provide homes for many exciting plants: vines, *Solanum crispum* in clouds of blue and the yellow cones of *Piptanthus laburnifolius*. The little *Convolvulus mauritanicus*, not quite hardy, is almost perpetual flowering.

A path down to the lake leads first to the shrub rose garden and the orange border beyond, where many plants with yellow flowers, yellowish foliage and autumn colour are to be found. Most subtle of the yellow foliage (at least in terms of yellowness!) are the variegated phormiums represented in several places through the garden in good forms.

An enormous *Platanus orientalis* (so picturesque yet so rarely seen) overhangs the beautiful wooden bridge across the lake, here narrowing and beginning to wind through the garden. The water garden is splendid from early spring with the spathes of lysichitums until autumn when ligularia and lobelia give way to autumn foliage and the free-flowering but invasive *Polygonum polystachyum*. The handsome group of *Cercidiphyllum japonicum* was planted in 1939.

The little church is well worth a visit and leads back to 'Westonbirt', much less spacious than its namesake but planted with many young trees, from magnolias to privets. Paths wind through the rich planting of the east pleasure garden back to the lake from whence the best view of the main shrub border is obtained. This was planted only in 1963 and already requires thinning. Many sorbus, a large *Magnolia x leobneri* and handsome groups of *Viburnum x hillieri* provide a backing for smaller shrubs. A young *Koelreuteria paniculata* at the foot of the border is already flowering. After fine views from the top of the border one can look more closely at the large shrubs from the narrow path behind the border, coming down again to the lake, the variegated bed and the walnut bed where the beautiful *Kirengeshoma palmata* flourishes in a much more open position than is usually given. The huge black walnut which gave this part of the garden its name fell dramatically in 1972 but its size may be gauged by the uneven canopies of the beech trees which surrounded it. A young walnut was planted in 1960 in anticipation of the fall and the area left vacant was planted with semi-mature beech in 1975.

From the open garden the path leads into light woodland past a curious 'leap-frog' beech which has layered its branches and a layer has layered itself in turn. A small glade of *Acer palmatum* forms leads to an enormous London Plane, with the second largest girth in Britain. The plane marks the head of the lake and there remains but a short walk past the temple, into Lady Emily's Garden with its predominantly blue/lavender colours and along the herbaceous border to the entrance and plant sales area. Many interesting plants are propagated from the garden and sold at prices which would shame the more mundane garden centres.

The Rectory, Barton-le-Clay, Beds

2 acres; no gardener; clay soil. Open once in July for GS. 6 miles N of Luton. From A6 in Barton-le-Clay, take Hitchin road (B655) and turn right into Church road.

The Rectory garden is quite flat but is high enough to offer attractive rural views. Also the moat on two sides provides a change of level and changes of character from dark and shady to open sunny banks. The immediate surrounds of the Tudor house are varied. To the north, near the entrance, are stables from which comes much useful peaty manure. To the east is a small rose garden. On the west side is a 'woodland dell' in miniature and along the south front is a narrow border for tender plants, overlooking the main lawn.

The open slope from lawn to moat is occupied by a rockery which fits most appropriately into the undulations of the bank. Grey-leaved plants thrive in this well-drained part of the garden, and show up exceptionally well against the dark wall of vegetation across the moat.

Within the mature framework of house, trees, moat and lawn, many new plants have been established since 1971. East of the main lawn, screened by old yew and beech, is a new grove of birch, cherry and lilac. Water plants grow along the moat, part of which is shallow enough for a bog garden, and the banks are particularly interesting. The need to screen an adjacent footpath while retaining more distant views provides an excuse for experimental planting, pruning and moving about of new shrubs and trees including several shrub roses and, perhaps most unusual of all, a thriving young *Cornus florida* 'Tricolor'.

Rest Hill Farm, Over Worton, Oxon

4 acres; 1 gardener; alkaline clay-loam over limestone. Open once in June or July for NGS. 7 miles S of Banbury. 2½ miles W of A423 (Oxford–Banbury) through Duns Tew or 2 miles N of B4030 (Bicester–Enstone) from Middle Barton.

The buildings of Rest Hill Farm are grouped around an open court, a pattern typical in the Cotswolds to provide shelter from the incessant wind. In the garden, too, walls and hedges have been placed to create a series of sheltered garden compartments. Apart from a few old apple trees and a walnut, the garden has been planted entirely since 1963, following the virtual rebuilding of the farmhouse.

An avenue of Turkey oaks along the drive, massed with daffodils, opens into the former rickyard, now planted with interesting trees including all six hardy species of *Aesculus* and the bold-leaved *Paulownia*. *Eucryphia x nymansensis* flourishes by the entrance to the yard and roses tumble over the roofs, while a raised peat bed accommodates the few calcifuge plants to be found here.

The main garden is south of the house. A semi-circular yew hedge and a hornbeam hedge along the south boundary, planted in 1963 and 1964 respectively, are pierced only once to frame a fine parkland view. Small sheltered gardens have been created between the two hedges.

To the west is a rose garden, with a swimming pool beyond. Built in 1966, the pool is enclosed by yew and pleached limes on the south, and on the north and west by stone walls which include a delightful traditional gazebo. The walls shelter many interesting climbers and, on the north side, they shade hydrangeas. To the east the hedges enclose a small garden of winter heathers and an herbaceous border in one of many gardens.

The main vista east of the central lawn extends between deep herbaceous borders to an informal pond made in 1970. Excavated material has been shaped into banks, and a series of smaller pools feed a waterfall into the pond. A summerhouse, built in 1971, and the fine walnut beside it terminate the vista. Before the terminus, curved hedges back rose-bordered walks to right and left. To the right, the walk emerges beneath an old apple at the top of the stream. To the left it leads to a circular tapestry hedge around a wellhead. Openings lead again to the water garden or to an area of varied specimen trees separating the pleasure garden from the tennis court and vegetables. These trees extend around the water garden whilst clematis and roses scramble through apple trees in the old farm orchard.

The idea for the tapestry hedge came from Hidcote Manor, and Rest Hill Farm is in many ways reminiscent of this famous garden, with sheltering hedges creating settings in which interesting plants can be carefully arranged to their best advantage.

Rooks Nest, Lambourn Woodlands, Berks

2½ acres; 1 gardener; thin chalk soil. Open once in June for NGS. 4½ miles N of Hungerford, 3 miles from junction 14 of M4. Signposted from Ermine Street just E of B4001.

There was no garden at Rooks Nest until 1929, when the sixteenth-century house was skilfully enlarged. In the early 1930s a stone wall was built along the road and yew hedges were planted to subdivide the garden and create shelter and interest on this flat, high and exposed site. Slight changes in level were increased by mounding the two curved borders in the main garden and emphasized by gradation of plant heights.

The garden is now a series of interlocking rectangles well furnished with interesting plants; even the farmyard is neat and colourful with pleached planes, hedges of rugosa roses and wall plants. The one area with marked changes of level is in the north corner of the garden. Probably an old chalk-pit, this corner is informal with bulbs massed in rough grass among specimen plants including *Cornus florida* 'Rubra', variegated *Liriodendron* and Blue Cedar.

The short lime avenue is now pleached and through it there is a colourful peep under an old yew to the main flower garden with opposing borders of soft and bold colours.

In recent years the garden has been simplified to keep it within the abilities of one gardener. The tennis court in the west corner, now unused, has many interesting shrubs and trees including some Italian

Cypress (*C.sempervirens*) grown from seed brought back from Italy. The old vegetable garden has been grassed down and planted with various sorbus and maples around a central deodar cedar. The new vegetable garden, behind a beech hedge, has also been halved by planting a new deep shrub border using pieces from elsewhere in the garden.

Not least of the attractions of Rooks Nest is the central courtyard, stone paved with an enormous water tank beneath the wellhead. The varied walls illustrate the architectural history of the house as well as carrying several well-established wall plants.

Rosemary House, Stanford-in-the-Vale, Oxon

½ acre; no gardener; shallow limestone brash. Open once in June for NGS. 5 miles NW of Wantage. From A417 (Wantage–Faringdon) turn E into Stanford village. House next to church.

Rosemary House was built in 1964 and the garden has been made subsequently from an open field. Walls extending from the house or standing free within and around the garden provide a variety of situations in a garden which is already full, varied and interesting throughout the year.

The courtyard is simply planted with birch and mahonia, in contrast to the brighter colours of the main garden where roses, narrow herbaceous borders and shrubs surround an informal lawn. A tiny pool and stream add to the interest while well-placed seats offer views of the garden and church. There are two obvious openings from the lawn: one leads to the small walled enclosure almost concealed by the shrubs while the other, much narrower, path winds around the pool and behind the walled garden as a miniature 'woodland walk' of hazel, birch and pine.

The paths converge again in the furthermost corner of the garden then wind along a dense shrub border to a second smaller lawn. Sequoia, metasequoia and other conifers stand among many shrubs planted for foliage colour in the foreground, while the background is thickened with more neutral shrubs, Lawson's cypress and birch. A large island of heathers is sensibly restricted to varieties of *Erica herbacea*

(*E.carnea*) which tolerates lime, but a raised peat bed near the house allows calcifuges to be grown, adding still further interest to the garden.

Rousham House, Steeple Aston, Oxon

30 acres; 2 gardeners; clay-loam soil. Open every day 10–6 (House open Apr–Sept only, Wed, Sun and Bank Hols, 2–5.30). See HHCG. 12 miles N of Oxford, E of A423 (Oxford–Banbury) at Hopcrofts Holt Hotel.

Rousham House was built for Sir Robert Dormer in 1635 and wings designed by William Kent were added in 1740. The garden was designed by Charles Bridgeman *c*.1715–1720 and altered by William Kent in succeeding decades. It escaped the 'improving hand' of Lancelot Brown and the attention of Victorian planters and so remains Kent's most complete work. It is not only of historical interest however: the walled gardens east of the house have many attractive features. A wide border of roses and herbaceous plants occupies the entire south wall of the main kitchen garden and part of the east wall, framing a pointed arch to the present much smaller vegetable garden. Trained apples and a central dipping pond remain to outline the quartered plan of the garden which has otherwise been grassed over. To the south is the narrower Pigeon House Garden with its circular stone pigeon house towering over a delightful box-edged rose garden. Box also screens the frame-yard at one end of the garden while the greenhouse and dahlia border lead beyond the pigeon house to the church and vegetable garden below.

Bridgeman's design for the main garden is generally formal and introvert but serpentine walks are apparent and the vistas are more loosely arranged than hitherto, dictated perhaps by the very irregular shape of the garden sloping north from the house to the small winding River Cherwell. Kent loosened the stiffness, opened vistas to more distant prospects where these could be obtained and added many architectural features.

The main vista extends northwards across Bridgeman's bowling green to Scheemaker's statue of a lion and horse on the skyline. To the west, paths wind between the ha-ha and river, past the 'Dying

Gladiator' to Venus' Vale, a wide vista extending to the river with a series of ponds and grotto-like cascades. A serpentine rill winds into the wood to the gloomy 'Cold Bath' and walks, both formal and irregular, follow similar routes to combine at the gigantic statue of Apollo. From here the garden is more open with Apollo and Kent's 'Temple of Echo' overlooking Heyford Bridge.

East of Venus' Vale are other classical features: the arched and vaulted Praeneste, Bridgeman's theatre, the lion and horse seen this time from below, and a pyramid by Kent. From this heavy stone temple below the walled garden, a path curves up through the dense screen back to the bowling green and house.

Royal National Rose Society Garden, Chiswell Green, Herts

12 acres; 4–5 gardeners; gravel soil. Open mid-June–end Sept, Mon–Sat 9–5; Sun 2–6. Close Aug Bank Hol Mon. Between Watford (4 miles) and St Albans (7 miles) turn E off A412 at the 'Three Hammers Inn', Chiswell Green, then ¾ mile.

The Bone Hill gardens were designed to display the enormous diversity of the genus *Rosa* and to test new varieties of rose being developed for commerce. Although the site is not conducive to either purpose, being flat and open with poor, gravelly soil, the Society has succeeded admirably since it moved here from Oaklands in 1960.

Near the entrance on the north side, a semicircle of pillar roses gives valuable height to the garden. The path then leads between beds of floribunda roses to a rotunda almost engulfed in *Rosa longicuspis*. It continues to a handsome pergola around a pool to return northwards on the other side of the office building. Both pergola and pool margin are decorated with more roses. The height and subdivision of the garden which these features provide are reinforced by columns of green and gold yew from the house to the pool (plants pre-dating the rose garden), and by the Henry Edland Memorial Pavilion which, with a long hedge of rugosa roses, separates the garden proper from the trial ground. Other plants, especially conifers, have also been added to furnish the garden more permanently.

Within this framework of permanent features and wide paths the great wealth of roses is displayed. Climbing roses have been mentioned already. At the other end of the scale is a sunken garden of miniature roses made on the west side of the garden in 1973. Raised borders display the tiny flowers with herbaceous plants to suggest suitable plant associations. The theme of plant association is developed in the adjacent small garden, designed by Society members. Between this and the service yard, the visitors' lounge has its own garden of favourite roses, including some tender ones on the south-facing wall.

Two main axes, the Princess Mary Rose Walk from the house and the wider vista from the Memorial Pavilion, allow larger scale massing of hybrid tea and floribunda roses but on either side of the latter vista, in the south-east and north-east corners of the garden, the planting is informal. Here are the increasingly popular 'Old Roses', gallicas and centifolias, damasks and Bourbons, Portlands and newer rugosas, grouped in irregular beds with winding grass walks among them. On the south-east edge, species and near species add variety of foliage, flower and fruit to the heavy perfumes of the old roses.

The trial ground, west of the main garden, is purely functional. Some 200–250 new roses are sent for trial each year by professional and amateur breeders and plants spend three years in the trial ground. Because of the poor soil, 100 tons of farmyard manure per acre is worked into the beds prior to planting. The first year is allowed for establishment. Assessment by a panel of 20 judges begins in the second year when a Trial Ground Certificate may be awarded to promising cultivars. In the third year a Certificate of Merit or Gold Medal is awarded to outstanding roses. Every care is given to the roses but in the second and third years, spraying stops in June to allow assessment of disease susceptibility. The trial borders are used on a ten-year rotation to prevent rose sickness, being grassed down when not in use to build up organic matter.

Every cultivar receiving an award since 1963 is planted in a long border round the perimeter of the trial ground, and it need hardly be said that all the roses are clearly labelled and expertly maintained.

St Nicholas, Wallingford, Oxon

2 acres; 1 gardener; alkaline, flinty soil much altered by building. Open once in August for NGS. 100 yards N of traffic lights in centre of Wallingford, on A329 to Oxford.

St Nicholas has a long history. Pre-Norman defences formed the basis for a castle built by William the Conqueror after his crossing of the Thames. The priory of St Nicholas within the ruins was suppressed in the sixteenth century and the castle was finally destroyed by Cromwell. The remains of the castle and priory form a picturesque backdrop to the garden.

The main garden is almost flat with borders of roses, paeonies, annuals and herbaceous plants around rectangular lawns. There are also several interesting shrubs planted by the owners since 1957. A young *Eucryphia x* 'Nymansay' usually produces its masses of white flowers for the open day. Beyond the flower garden are the vegetables and a long cutting border backed by an ancient yew hedge. Below part of the old wall, a tunnel leads to the keep where planting is informal.

Following heavy losses from Dutch Elm Disease, the steep mound of the castle keep has been gradually cleared and replanted, covering the great mound with colourful shrubs. Gardening is not easy on this steep, dry slope but considerable progress has been made and it is interesting to be able to look into the tops of tall shrubs from the path which spirals to the top of the mound.

St Paul's Walden Bury, Whitwell, Herts

75 acres; 2 gardeners; neutral boulder clay. Open four times in April, May, June for GS, NGS etc, or by arrangement. On B651 (St Albans–Hitchin) 5 miles S of Hitchin, 1½ miles N of Whitwell.

The garden of St Paul's Walden Bury has been aptly described as a 'Grand Garden in Miniature' and is a wonderful example of the variety and surprise which can be achieved within a formal layout, including much of horticultural interest.

North of the house the lawn, bordered by pleached limes, terminates in a woodland alcove against which stand two Van Nost statues of wrestlers. The woodland is penetrated by three radiating rides lined throughout by beech hedges. The central vista, 600 yards long, emphasizes the undulation of the garden by its very straightness and focuses on a large statue of Hercules. To the east, one diagonal ride extends to the church and to the west a shorter vista terminates at a statue in the woodland. All three are connected repeatedly by lateral rides extending into the countryside or terminating at a statue or temple. Within the segments of woodland formed by the network of walks are various enclosed gardens.

The woodland was laid out by Edward Gilbert *c.*1725–30 but it comes as a surprise to find that this gem of formal gardening, relying so much on vistas, architecture and sculpture, owes its continued existence to the late President of the Royal Horticultural Society. Soon after the Hon. David Bowes Lyon moved to St Paul's Walden in 1932 he began replanting the miles of beech hedge, renewing avenues and restoring the garden, rescuing features from many less fortunate gardens in so doing. The round temple terminating the west end of the first cross-axis came from Copped Hall, Essex. At the other end of the vista, between the fishpond and stew-ponds which pre-date the garden by many centuries, is Sir William Chambers' temple designed for Danson Park, Kent now looking very much at home reflected in the pond. The theatre garden between the two lateral rides was reinstated by Mr Bowes Lyon and Geoffrey Jellicoe although the temple and discus thrower were already there.

Despite its architectural formality, the garden is certainly not without flowers and horticultural interest. West of the theatre garden is a rhododendron garden with many plants brought from the Himalayas. Near the house the woodland opens to a small, more formal flower garden west of the main lawn. On the east side a terrace overlooks an extensive informal garden framing the pool and Chambers' temple. Paths wind through wide mixed borders where shrubs, herbaceous plants, annuals and bulbs thrive in well-planned associations. often reflected in the pond.

Salisbury Hall, London Colney, Herts

1 acre; part-time gardener; gravel soil. Open Suns 2–6 Easter–Sept; and Thurs 2–6 July–Sept and Bank Hols, 10.30–5.30. See HHCG. 5 miles S of St Albans on A6.

The site of Salisbury Hall is exactly square, of exactly one acre and surrounded by an acre of moat. It may well have been a Roman outpost, was built on in the 9th century, moated in the eleventh and the present manor house is seventeenth-century.

A fine brick bridge crosses the moat and the drive is then bordered by a yew hedge planted by Lady Randolph (Jennie) Churchill in 1905. Links with the Churchills are continued beyond the moat at the back of the house where, in an old lime tree, one can still see the tree house built by the gardener for Winston Churchill. Also beyond the moat are the prototype aircraft which, with the Hall itself, are the main attractions.

The garden itself, the remnant of a Victorian layout, is not a major feature although the front part is neat and colourful. With the moat and wide gravel forecourt it forms a delightful setting for a most interesting house. Indeed, successive archaeological excavations and a plethora of remaining foundations almost preclude any further development of the garden.

Sarratt Gardens, Herts

Four gardens on acid gravel over chalk. Open once in late May/June for RC. *Old Rectory* is also open for NGS. Gardens are in Church Lane, Sarratt, 7 miles NW of Watford. From North Orbital Road (A412) take Chorleywood exit then second signposted turning right to Sarratt.

Greystokes (2 acres; ½ gardener): The garden was made, with the older part of the house, in 1930. A walled rose garden is the principal feature but there is also a rockery-bordered pool and a swimming pool within the considerable length of the garden, while crab apples and flowering cherries are scattered informally in the long grass.

A new wing was added to the house in 1975 together with a curved wall to shelter a wide and handsome terrace. A vegetable garden has been established and other changes are likely, including perhaps a new swimming pool garden within the rose garden, replacing the old-fashioned and inconveniently sited old pool.

Little Nobles (⅓ acre excl. large drive; no gardener): The house was converted from the garage and mews of the adjacent older house in 1965 and the garden was begun at the same time, although it incorporates some plants of the older garden. It is an enthusiast's garden, made even more attractive by its woodland setting.

The approach from the east is by a gravel drive winding between old shrubs concealing the stables. The narrow side entrance is heavily shaded but thickly planted with ferns, hellebores, small bulbs and much more, opening to a curved terrace below banks of heathers. A rose garden forms the central feature of the lawn. On the south side are apples, vegetables and a small formal garden of herbs and grey-leaved plants. On the north side is a curving and very flourishing border of small shrubs including several azaleas. The two sides curve to meet at the small greenhouse in which many of the plants growing in the house and garden are propagated for sale on open days.

Nobles (1½ acres; part-time gardener): The garden was begun in 1905. The orchard underplanted with bulbs provides an informal entrance to the front lawn bordered by magnolias, rhododendrons and cherries. To the south is a new vegetable garden, beyond the tennis court and outside the garden proper. The main garden, south-west of the house against a background of beech and oak woods, is flat and sheltered.

From the terrace there is a walk between borders of roses and herbaceous plants. The swimming pool, across the garden, has its own sunken paved garden partly concealed by the old conifers, apples and new shrubs in the intervening lawn. At the end of the garden is a rock garden of separate island beds in the lawn. This feature, added in 1973, is already well established with heathers, low shrubs and dwarf conifers merging into the woodland background.

The Old Rectory (2½ acres; 1 gardener): This spacious garden is note-worthy for its great variety of hedges enclosing the garden on three sides, leaving the fourth side open to exploit the fine view over the Chess valley. Dense holly borders the orchard in the upper part of the garden. Pleached lime and columns of golden yew encircle the drive with its island of shrub roses while a low lavender hedge borders the path to the main door.

From the main terrace, the radial pattern of which is echoed by paths cut through the long grass of the open slope, there are panoramic views flanked by further hedges. To the left, hornbeam, rugosa roses and an old field hedge extend from the drive to the edge of the ha-ha. To the right is a pleached lime walk leading to a summerhouse which again enjoys fine views. Near the terrace, the limes terminate at sentinel pines from which point a yew hedge curves round an azalea border and low catalpa, creating a shaded alcove on the otherwise open terrace.

Extending from the long axis of the house is a swimming pool within a double beech hedge. Four pairs of silver-leaved pear frame the en-trances to this elliptical enclosure, leading out on the three sides away from the house into an informal shrub garden and hence into walks through established and newly planted woodlands.

Sarsden Glebe, Churchill, Oxon

---

3 acres; 1 gardener/handyman; ironstone brash soil. Open once in April and July for NGS. 3 miles SW of Chipping Norton, on B4450. From Burford take A361 and turn W for Churchill.

The forecourt of this 1820 rectory is simple and beautiful. From the gate a grass bank rises to form a sheltering bowl merging into banks of ever-greens over the tunnel-like back drive. The lofty east doorway is reduced to a low cavern by long trails of winter jasmine. A small gate leads to a low border of grey foliage and pastel flowers, an open grass terrace and thence to the garden proper, west of the house.

An arching laburnum frames the entrance to the wild garden inviting exploration but a better route is to descend the steep steps through a spring shrub border to a secluded lawn then down again through a shrub rose border to the lower lawn and herbaceous border. Both lawns end by a large beech which marks the transition from terracing to natural slopes. A further very gentle descent opens to a large rectangle of rough grass with a small pool backed by a spinney of larch and pine. Open views to the left contrast to the earlier enclosure and the wild garden is to the right.

This is shaded by large beech and oaks with an understorey of attractive shrubs. In spring there are carpets of bulbs, especially *Anemone blanda* and in autumn *Cyclamen* (*neapolitanum*) appear in large numbers.

Quite separate from this main garden is the walled kitchen garden with a narrow border on the outside of two walls. Approached by a few steep steps (but visible from the drive) the long border is rich in old-fashioned roses and the short border has an herbaceous border with many spring-flowering cushions in the dry wall along the path.

Savill Garden, Windsor, Berks see Windsor Great Park.

Shinfield Grange, Shinfield, Berks (University of Reading)

15 acres; 4 gardeners; sandy gravel over clay. Open once each month May–Oct for GS, NGS and other charities. Plant sales. 3 miles S of Reading off A327 (Reading–Aldershot) just S of M4 crossing, turn E into Cutbush Lane then ½ mile.

This seventeenth-century farmhouse, considerably enlarged in 1857, was bought by the University of Reading in 1949 and converted into laboratories with a teaching garden for horticulture students. The site is low lying and poorly drained on the east side, sloping gradually to a shallow depression in the south where a small lake has been formed. Minor variations in soil type and the presence of several large trees have influenced the arrangement of the garden.

Much of the early development took place in the partly walled kitchen garden after planting a hornbeam hedge to enclose its south and east sides. With the extension of research glasshouses into this area (which is not open to the public) these early borders were replaced on a larger scale elsewhere in the garden. A wide range of plants has been assembled and in recent years propagation from this collection has allowed bolder groupings to unify the garden and establish a variety of situations from colourful beds and formal borders near the house to a more natural long grass and wild flowers in the outlying parts of the garden.

The drive curves between trees, grass and bulbs to the north front of the house where shade plants fill the narrow border. Hornbeams and a large oak frame the north lawn on which the heather garden begins. There are fine groups of the tall *Erica arborea* 'Alpina' as well as lower ericas beneath witchhazel, *Cornus mas*, azaleas and other shrubs. The large oak, strategically sited on a slight ridge, marks the entrance to a long glades. Limes, oaks and a large walnut frame this tapering vista bordered by heathers, rhododendrons, cornus and associated plants for spring flower and autumn colour. The soil here is more acid than elsewhere in the garden.

The Long Walk, south of the glade is bordered by *Berberis*, *Viburnum*, *Cotoneaster* and other important shrubby genera. The botanical grouping here is useful but the borders are being enlarged and diversified to provide more variety of form. The new yew hedges planted to the west in 1977 and a cherry garden to the east, planted in 1975, link the long walk to other parts of the garden.

Picea brewerana terminates the main walk. Beyond it the ground is too wet to permit direct access to the lake, so mown paths turn to right and left around the willow collection to reach the lake bank by higher ground. Planting around the lake is limited to allow views of and over the water. One such view is to the rock garden at the west end of the lake, on a promontory made with topsoil removed during construction of the Plant Environment Laboratory. The many conifers in the rock garden increase its height and separate it from the shade garden beyond.

The shade garden was enlarged in 1973 after moving the metasequoia to a more open position, and it has a varied collection of hostas, ferns, primulas, rodgersias etc. To the west is a small collection of sorbus and other trees through which a mown ride leads to the Summer Borders. In these beech- and hornbeam-hedged gardens there are rectangular borders for the display of annuals and tender perennials of various types, including a fine border of foliage plants. The layout of the Summer Borders was altered in 1975/6 to allow direct access to the June Garden of irises, paeonies, roses, clematis and other June flowers.

The herbaceous border north of the June Garden is planted in a deep curve between flowering cherries to the south and large shrubs to the north. An island herbaceous border and borders of hebe and legumes on the adjacent well-drained ridge enclose paths which also curve northwards to the house.

The south terrace, made in 1951, provides a sheltered situation for tender plants, including climbers on the pergola at its western end. However, wall space is limited and, after the removal of a large acacia and *Magnolia grandiflora* in 1976, the policy has been to replace plants frequently, before they become too large. East of the terrace is a rose garden surrounded by a horseshoe border of early and late flowering shrubs. Between rose garden and terrace is a small formal garden in which bedding schemes can be displayed on a modest scale.

South of these hedged gardens is a new enclosure, planted in 1977 to reduce the scale of the otherwise open expanses of grass. This new hedge and a second large walnut, with the herbaceous borders to the west, frame a shallow valley of rough grass down to the more natural margins of the lake.

Sluice Cottage, Wendover, Bucks

$2\frac{1}{2}$ acres; part-time gardener; chalk soil. Open once in July for GS. Immediately S of Wendover off A413 in Church Lane (opposite parish church).

The main garden of Sluice Cottage borders the drive and continues, past the cottage perched on the edge of a pool, to an irregular small garden of roses and herbaceous plants. The chief interest lies in old roses and very fine delphiniums although these are supported by bearded iris, lupin, philadelphus and Michaelmas daisy in due season. This small 'cottagey' garden is separated from the much larger orchard by two streams which meet at the sluice. One flows through the garden; the other originates within the garden in a shady spring-fed hollow of considerable charm.

Near the bridge leading over to the cottage some of the old fruit trees have been removed and others furnished with climbing roses to unite orchard and garden but not to the extent of diluting the colour of the garden or shady wilderness of the more distant parts of the orchard.

Southill Park, Biggleswade, Beds

11 acres; 3 gardeners; sandy soil. Open once in July for NGS. 5 miles SW of Biggleswade, W of B658 (Sandy–Shefford) through Southill village.

Southill Park shows evidence of at least three generations of keen gardeners around the house remodelled for the family by Henry Holland in 1795. From the north terrace there are glimpses of a landscape garden by Holland's eminent father-in-law 'Capability' Brown. *This is not open to the public* but there are several fine beech and holm oak of Brown's era in the flower garden. Most remarkable is a huge beech on the east side: it has layered itself to form a forest of trunks around the majestic hub.

The house, also opened, has its conservatory on the east end festooned with the tender rose 'La Folette'. From the house the main feature is a circular rose garden, an important focal point restored by the present owner. Its axis leads south through an alley of rhododendrons framing views of the parkland beyond.

To the west an informal vista from the rose garden follows a new purple border (partially concealing the present vegetable garden) to the ha-ha with views of the park framed between cedars. A group of beech conceal the swimming pool, tennis court, and an older abandoned court which has been planted with heathers. To the east the rose garden axis extends past the conservatory and large herbaceous beds to centre on a pergola stepping down the slope.

The east garden is generally mature: large *Arbutus* and *Liquidambar* lead to the layered beech, Holm Oaks and yew. Within their shadows is a sunken circle of brick walls with steps leading upwards in sinuous curves between grass banks (probably the remains of a rock-strewn dell) to the rhododendron alley. At the very edge of the east garden, a small elm copse, killed by Dutch Elm Disease, has been cleared to create a spring garden of flowering trees and bulbs: an encouraging sight as few gardens of this age show such obvious signs of continuing development.

Stanstead Lodge, Stanstead Abbots, Herts

2 acres; part-time help; clay soil near river, gravel above with much of the garden on old foundations. Open twice in June/July for RC, NSPCC. 2 miles E of Stanstead Abbots on A414 (Hertford–Harlow).

Stanstead Lodge was skilfully enlarged in 1965 after a fire which removed the surrounding old farm buildings. Except for a group of birch (still showing fire damage) and a few isolated plants, the garden developed subsequently. The outline of the garden is simple, in keeping with the now elegant house, but there are many interesting plants.

From the forecourt with its low wall festooned with roses, a large *Cytisus battandieri* conceals the main garden. The open lawn, slightly terraced, is bounded by a sinuous border with many good shrubs, low enough in places to reveal views over surrounding farmland. A tall mixed hedge encloses the west boundary (the top of the garden) while on the north side a hedge of modern shrub roses planted in 1974 separates the lawn and vegetable garden.

The walls of the house itself support many plants including a Banksian Rose (older, even, than the birch trees), the *Cytisus* and Corsican Rosemary on the south face, and *Ribes speciosum. Piptanthus laburnifolius* and *Phygelius capensis* on the west. Roses, clematis and *Hydrangea petiolaris* lead round to the front of the house, cream washed and a splendid background for red roses, grape and more clematis.

From this approach the entrance to the pool gardens (planted in 1972) is obvious, tucked away near the birch trees. In this very dry corner *Cistus, Hebe, Potentilla, Convolvulus cneorum* and other low shrubs are flourishing.

Beyond the garden proper, a gift of 25 silver birch for the owners' silver wedding anniversary forms the nucleus of a new planting with *Aruncus dioicus (sylvester) Cornus alba* and other waterside plants along the river bank.

Steart Hill House, Little Horwood, Bucks

3 acres; 1 gardener; clay soil. Open Suns and Bank Hols, May–Sept, 2–6. Plant sales. 400 yards S of A421 between Buckingham (6 miles) and Bletchley (4½ miles) on road to Mursley *not* Little Horwood. See HHCG.

In 1954 Steart Hill had one apple tree and a pear tree. These are still there but the formerly bare hillside is now a flourishing garden impressive for its variety and high standard of maintenance. Its main feature is roses but these are not grown at the expense of other plants: the wide range of plants and their skilful grouping offer valuable lessons for owners of even the smallest gardens.

Long shrub borders flank the open lawn at the entrance and two more borders line the courtyard around which the house is arranged. *Rosa rubrifolia*, *Berberis thunbergii* 'Atropupurea' and *Hippophae rhamnoides*, included in these borders, occur throughout the garden and exemplify the many good foliage plants used.

An unusual feature is the greenhouse with a long pool surrounded by bananas, cannas and other exotic foliage. A fuchsia-filled conservatory leads out into the 'old-fashioned' garden where a path lined with lavender, pinks and iris opens onto an old rose border and a small irregular glade. This small corner illustrates the success of close planting: the absence of large trees is not felt and, as throughout the garden, there are many examples of colour grouping in flower and foliage.

In the adjacent walled garden, the outdoor swimming pool is set off-centre and surrounded by narrow herbaceous borders. Outside the walls, the sloping glade narrows between the end of the pool garden and the boundary of young willows, beneath which are many plants tolerant of dry shady conditions. The shade emphasizes the bright colours of the rose garden around the corner: climbing roses on the wall are balanced by large shrub roses hanging over from the bank below while beds of modern roses fill the centre of the rose garden. Gaps between the shrub roses allow views of the countryside, and the terrace .at the end of the rose garden gives a panoramic view of fields, woods and water across the ha-ha. However, this direction leads away from one of the most successful of all the colour groupings so it is better to walk back along the rose garden and to continue down the hill. At the beginning of the winding path, foliage colours contrast: the dark green of *Viburnum davidii* and *Elaeagnus pungens* with white and silver of *Cornus alba* 'Elegantissima' and *Hippophae*. Further down the colours soften until, against the deepest purple berberis, a bright spot of yellow acts as a focal point. On closer investigation this reveals a small yellow garden. Several paths lead through this planting to the main lawn, the ha-ha and the shrub rose bank already seen from above. At the far end of the lawn another dense planting, with many evergreen shrubs for maximum screening in a minimum depth, has paths winding through into the orchard.

At the furthest corner from the house a small triangular spinney planted mainly with willows and poplars in 1967 is now well established, and groups of cornus and the wilder roses are beginning to spread beneath them. With further planting of bulbs and other low plants this will soon be a most attractive natural corner, complementing the more colourful parts of the garden.

Beyond the orchard a small herb garden and vegetable garden lead full circle back to the courtyard and stall from which plants propagated in the garden are sold.

Stoke Court, Stoke Poges, Bucks

23 acres; 2 gardeners; gravel soil over clay. Open once in Aug for GS. $2\frac{1}{2}$ miles N of Slough in Roger's Lane, off Bell's Hill, Stoke Poges.

The sixteenth-century 'West End House' was renamed 'Stoke Court' after alterations by Granville John Penn in 1845. It was used as a Country Club from 1927 to 1953 and now houses the offices and laboratories of Miles Laboratories Ltd.

The garden is a blend of old and new. The main entrance was planted with shrubs by Waterers *c*.1960 and the wide borders are now well established and virtually weed-proof. South west of the house is the rose-planted terrace, looking south over a formal garden enclosed by a low wall built by the Penns. The small informal lake beyond is the first of a chain extending outside the modern boundary. From the west end of the terrace a large magnolia and handsome yew hedge frame the beginning of a gravel walk above the formal garden, bordered on the upper side by tall shrubs including several rhododendrons.

The remaining garden is open but historically interesting. The garden is scattered with beech, plane and chestnut, all about 250 years old. The oak-lined walk, replanted by Miles Laboratories Ltd. since 1963, is associated with Thomas Gray who wrote his famous Elegy in the nearby Stoke Poges churchyard. Until intervening trees grew too tall the Eton spires, mentioned in Gray's poems, could be seen from the eighteenth-century summerhouse, the remains of which can still be seen in the south-west corner of the walk. The fact that this walk existed in 1719 makes it an early example of the walks planned for distant prospects which were precursors of the informal landscape gardens later in the eighteenth century.

Stonehouse, Whitchurch, Bucks

$4\frac{1}{2}$ acres; $1\frac{1}{2}$ gardeners; clay soil. Open twice in Aug for GS, NGS. 5 miles N of Aylesbury on A413. In Whitchurch fork left onto Oving Road. First house on right after inn.

The immediate impression at Stonehouse is of neatness and colour: each year thousands of bedding plants are raised to create a vivid display. This is not a summer garden only, however. There are many features of interest throughout the year.

From the east side of the house a lawn extends beyond a formal rose garden to a border of spring-flowering shrubs planted in 1972. Along the roadside boundary is an autumn border of dahlias, cleome, salpiglossis etc. while the spring border has many evergreen plants of winter interest.

North of the house is a sunken paved area with a formal pool and curved steps leading up to the main vista. This is flanked on the left by a long flower bed and on the right by the main feature of the garden, a pergola backed by a tall beech hedge. Curving borders which envelope the pergola have shrubs and roses interplanted with many annuals.

The vista continues across a drive linking the stable-yard, paddocks and vegetable garden, and into a small beech grove planted *c.*1910. The origin of the steep hummocks on which the beech are planted remains a mystery but their undulations add much interest to the garden. In spring there is a carpet of early bulbs and in summer cool shade as a foil to the flower garden. A yew hedge conceals the vegetable garden.

In the east garden, by the spring border, a small flight of steps leads to the gardener's garden which is also opened. Its colourful flower beds and many dwarf conifers reflect the character of the main garden in miniature.

Stowe, Buckingham, Bucks (Stowe School)

250 acres; 10 groundsmen/gardeners; boulder clay soil. Open late March–late April and mid-July to early Sept, 10–6 daily. See HHCG. 3 miles N of Buckingham, signposted from A413 (Buckingham–Towcester) and A43 (Brackley–Towcester) but see below.

Stowe is not a garden in the horticultural sense of the word, although it does contain many fine trees, a guide to which is available. It has, however, played an important part in the history of the English Garden, employing the most notable architects and landscape gardeners of the eighteenth century in its development.

Simple directions to Stowe are given in the introduction, but a more dramatic approach is to go into the centre of Buckingham, turn towards Brackley then first right. The narrow lane passes between twin lodges and suddenly out of town. The avenue, now replanted, continues for over a mile to the triumphal Corinthian Arch. Through the arch the vista continues down to the Octagon Lake and up again to the great house. The main features of this plan were designed by Charles Bridgeman early in the 7120s and Bridgeman's deliberate use here of the sunken boundary wall or ha-ha created a turning point in garden design.

There is no access through the Corinthian Arch so it is necessary to continue on the main road to the entrance gates and between the Boycott Pavilions to the north front of the house. The house, built by Sir Richard Temple c.1680, was enlarged in the 1720s and 30s by his son (also Sir Richard, later Viscount Cobham) with Sir John Vanbrugh as chief architect. More important than his reshaping of the house was the simultaneous reshaping of the garden, because Bridgeman omitted the high walls which invariably surrounded earlier gardens in favour of a ha-ha giving distant prospects, and although the garden was largely formal, it was no longer symmetrical. Bridgeman seized on several existing features by using diagonal walks to incorporate them into the garden and his basic organization of the garden at Stowe remains unaltered.

The most significant of his successors was William Kent who designed many of the structures at Stowe as incidents in the picturesque landscape scenes which he created. Kent began by embellishing Bridgeman's open landscape with the Temple of Venus (*c.*1730) on the southern spur of the ha-ha, but soon turned to the more intimate scale of a small valley east of the house. Here he developed the Elysian Fields, a classical paradise with temples, monuments and other features seen one from another in carefully framed vistas until the awesome grotto at the head of the valley was reached. In 1975 work began on clearing dense growth prior to restoration of the crumbling structure, and the grotto will soon be a major re-addition to the garden.

Of the many buildings throughout the garden, one might single out for mention the Pebble Alcove, south of the Octagon Lake, by the tennis courts. The colourful pebble mosaic was restored in 1967 by Benjamin Gibbon and its motto, *Templa Quam Dilecta* (How Delightful are thy Temples), befits the creators of Stowe and their creation.

Kent continued to work at Stowe for nearly 20 years but in the latter years of his life it seems probable that improvements were left largely in the hands of Lord Cobham himself and his new head gardener, Lancelot ('Capability') Brown, appointed in 1741. Almost certainly the Grecian Valley north of the Elysian Fields was their work. It was the last major addition to the gardens. Brown left in 1751, following the deaths of Kent (1748) and Cobham (1749) to practise widely as an architect and landscape gardener.

When Earl Temple, Lord Cobham's nephew and successor, enlarged and aggrandized the house, the south front of the garden was opened and simplified to remain in scale. Then, after 70 years of creative activity, Stowe sank into obscurity, escaping the worst depredations of the Victorian era and only emerging from dormancy in 1923 when it became Stowe School.

The main changes which followed were centred around the house, where new school buildings have continued to be added to the present day. From the beginning, however, the importance of Stowe was recognized and efforts were made to restore both house and garden until war intervened in 1939. In 1965 a Landscape Committee was formed: Hugh Creighton, ARIBA reported on the state of the garden buildings and subsequently supervised a ten-year programme of restoration. In 1967 John Workman, Forestry Adviser to the National

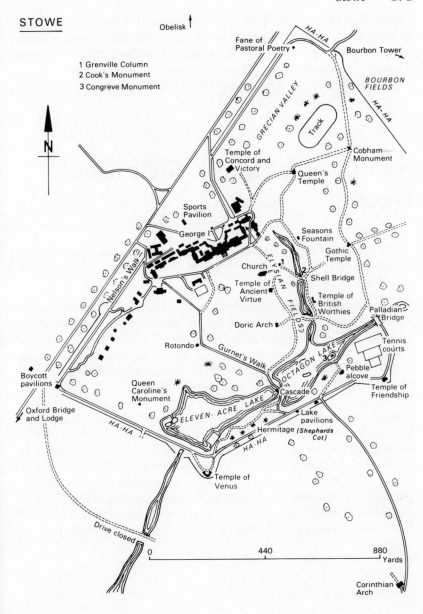

STOWE

1 Grenville Column
2 Cook's Monument
3 Congreve Monument

N

Obelisk

Fane of
Pastoral Poetry

HA-HA

Bourbon Tower

BOURBON
FIELDS

GRECIAN VALLEY

Track

HA-HA

Temple of
Concord and
Victory

Cobham
Monument

Queen's
Temple

Sports
Pavilion

George I

Seasons
Fountain

Gothic
Temple

Nelson's Walk

Church

ELYSIAN FIELDS

1

2

Shell Bridge

Temple of
Ancient
Virtue

Temple of
British
Worthies

Palladian
Bridge

Doric Arch

Tennis
courts

Rotondo

Gurnet's Walk

OCTAGON LAKE

3

Pebble
alcove

Boycott
pavilions

Temple of
Friendship

Queen
Caroline's
Monument

Cascade

Oxford Bridge
and Lodge

HA-HA

ELEVEN-ACRE LAKE

Lake
pavilions

Hermitage *(Shepherds Cot)*

HA-HA

Temple of
Venus

Drive closed

0   440   880
                                           Yards

Corinthian
Arch

Trust, drew up a similar plan for the woodlands. Restoration and improvement are evident throughout the garden and, although much remains to be done, visitors will be inspired as much by the work of those responsible for restoration as by the earlier vision of the Temple and Grenville families who created this 'earthly paradise'.

Swinbrook House, Swinbrook, Oxon

6 acres; 2 gardeners; limestone soil. Open once in July for NGS. 2 miles E of Burford, turn N off A40 to Swinbrook. Midway between Swinbrook and Shipton-under-Wychwood.

The present Swinbrook House was built *c.*1920 on a high site commanding wide views. The site is that of a much older house demolished in 1805, and the remains of its great formal garden are still clearly evident in the terracing of the grassy hillside south and west of the house. The hilltop is sheltered by tall beech and ash along the drive to the west and by orchard and woodland to the east.

The drive curves around the walls of the old kitchen garden and through the forecourt to a roundel of pillars. There is some formal gardening south of the rondel near the house but the main flower garden has been developed more recently, with great ingenuity, north of the house. The end wall of the kitchen garden has been lowered to reveal a herbaceous garden surrounded by a shrub border in which purple and grey foliage predominate. A new vegetable garden has been established outside the walls with glasshouses, tennis court, squash court and croquet lawn also fitting in to the pattern established by the paths.

Swinbrook Manor, Swinbrook, Oxon

1 acre; part-time gardener; clay-loam over limestone. Open once in July for NGS. 2 miles E of Burford, turn N off A40, then 1 mile.

This was originally the manor farm for the old Swinbrook Manor, which has now disappeared. The grouping of its buildings adds much charm to the garden, as do the numerous walls enclosing yards which are now part of the garden. The garden was planned c.1940 but became over-grown. The present owner has partly cleared the garden since 1971, retaining the best shrubs and trees. Walls have been repaired and new planting is almost complete.

A mixed border with an emphasis on good foliage plants has been established by the south-west corner of the house, separating the main lawn from a smaller lawn bounded by raised beds. The shelter and free drainage of these beds, high above the road, are ideal for grey-leaved plants. Shrub roses have been planted in a walled garden to the north west. The heathers on the terrace overlooking the courtyard received a severe setback in the drought of 1976 but the garden as a whole will grow in interest for many years.

Troy, Ewelme, Oxon

3 acres; 1 gardener; gravel soil. Open once in April and July for GS, NGS. 1 mile S of Ewelme, 1 mile N of A423 between Wallingford (2½ miles) and Henley-on-Thames (8 miles).

The garden at Troy is varied and interesting, with doves, hens and Jacob's sheep to add still more interest, especially for children. Along the drive a young avenue of walnuts, alternating with 'John Downie' crab apples for more immediate effect, is underplanted with bulbs. The drive enters the forecourt opposite a sunken herb garden, convenient to the kitchen and shaded in part by old apple trees. The forecourt is surrounded by clipped yews, two of which form entrance pillars to the small silver garden planted in 1972 at the end of the house.

Beyond the silver garden, the gentle west slope is terraced in two directions from the house, with a swimming pool in its own small sheltered garden balancing the terraces. The north-west garden, below a rockery bank, features shrub roses and bearded iris around a small pool, with tender shrubs against the house. There is also a tiny conservatory and laburnum-covered gazebo. To the south west is a large lawn, with a wide border of trees and newer shrubs on the west concealing the tennis court and orchard. Along the east boundary, large shrub groups balance the vista without impeding views over the farm. Similar planting continues among large apple trees to the vegetable garden.

Finally, between the vegetable garden and swimming pool is a remnant of the ha-ha which can be traced through the garden. From here, one has the closest view of the older summerhouse, mentioned by Jerome K. Jerome, to whom the house once belonged, in his autobiography.

Tudor Barn, Windsor, Berks

3½ acres; 3 part-time gardeners; clay soil. Open once in June for NGS. 2 miles from centre of Windsor, turn right off B3022 to St Leonard's Hill. House on right.

Tudor Barn is a twentieth-century house built around a seventeenth-century barn, more or less in the centre of its garden. Large oaks serve as reminders that this was once part of Windsor Forest and the clay soil has been modified by centuries of leaf-fall. The garden, developed since 1934, is open in character with plants of interest at all seasons.

The south lawn, screened from the road by rhododendrons and camellias, has several fine oaks framing views of the house from the sunken croquet lawn which is bordered by roses and hydrangeas. The thatched hut north of the croquet lawn is copied from African examples. It provides free air circulation ideal for storing produce, and so forms a logical link between the pleasure garden and the vegetables, cutting border, fruit and small greenhouse in the north-west quarter.

North of the house are twin herbaceous and rose borders. To the east, shrubs and crab apples extend along much of the boundary, concealing a second small vegetable garden in the north-east corner. This low, wet area is ideal for maincrops and for waterside ornamentals.

Perhaps the most attractive area is immediately east of the house where a formal pool lies in a hollow surrounded by a rock garden now overgrown with once-miniature shrubs. The changes of level building up to the dense planting of hydrangeas and fuchsias around the house is especially attractive when viewed through nearby trees.

As might be expected in a garden developed by one enthusiast for over 40 years, there is a rich mixture of bulbs, herbaceous plants, shrubs and roses. Particularly unusual are the fat clumps of *Eucomis bicolor*, a reputedly tender bulb which has multiplied without protection here for many years. Although ivies, *Euonymus* and other permanent plants are slowly replacing annuals in the many vases about the garden to save labour, new hardy plants indicate continuing interest.

Turville Court, Turville Heath, Bucks

4 acres; 1 gardener; acid sandy soil over chalk. Open once in June for NGS. 5 miles N of Henley-on-Thames. W of B480 (Henley–Watlington) on road from Stonor to Fingest.

Turville Court began as a small farmhouse, probably of Tudor origins. The garden was established *c.*1900 and, although now much simplified, much of its original plan remains. On this high spur with extensive views to the south and east, shelter is of great importance. The buildings are grouped around two yards, and sycamores on the north boundary provide not only a windbreak but a shaded walk in contrast to the open lawn. This windbreak and the kitchen garden to the south, below the lawn, frame views to the east.

The walls of the kitchen garden are screened by a tall overgrown shrubbery which, with similar plantings curving down from the house, frame the second major view to the south. A well-maintained rose garden terminates this axis but low steps to the west lead to a more sheltered garden above the orchard. The pergola in this secluded alcove was destroyed by gales in 1975 although some climbing plants still remain in the grass. A long herbaceous border backed by buddleias on the upper edge of the garden leads to a winding grass walk, past a shadowy pool and back to the house.

Valley Gardens, Windsor, Berks see Windsor Great Park

Waddesdon Manor, Waddesdon, Bucks (The National Trust)

160 acres; 7 gardeners plus 5 (max.) summer help; clay soil over chalk. Open Wed–Sat, 2–6; Sun 11.30–6 (House 2–6 only) and Bank Hols 11–6 from last Wed in Mar to last Sun in Oct. See HHCG. In centre of Waddesdon on S side of A41 between Aylesbury (6 miles) and Bicester (10 miles).

Waddesdon Manor is remarkable for the quality and quantity of its collections. Books, paintings, sculpture, china, furniture and furnishings, especially of the eighteenth century, are displayed in the great 'French château' designed by Gabriel-Hippolyte Destailleur and built in 1874–1889 for Baron Ferdinand de Rothschild. The exuberant collector's spirit of the nineteenth century also extends to the garden which was laid out by the French landscape gardener, Lainé.

He flattened the top of the bare hill to make a level expanse for the house and the formal approach. The trees, which are now such a feature of Waddesdon, were then brought in from the surrounding countryside, many of them fully grown. They were drawn into place by strong Percheron horses, imported from Flanders.

The gardens were further enriched with other trees and shrubs by Miss Alice de Rothschild, Baron Ferdinand's sister, and his successor at Waddesdon from 1898 to 1922.

The winding drive from the village arrives at the Triton Fountain then opens into the main platform with five parallel avenues to the north façade of the house. The parterre to the south, centred on the eighteenth-century Fountain of Pluto and Proserpine, is equally impressive. 7,000 plants are required to fill the beds, tulips and wallflowers in the spring, geraniums and ageratum in the summer.

Steps and vistas radiate from the level expanse surrounding the house which merges into a fine example of informal Victorian gardening. Winding paths criss-cross the hillside among specimen trees, shrubs and sculpture. In the north-west corner of the approach, spectacular rock-work borders the path to the aviary. The aviary itself, contemporary with the house, strikes a formal note with neat hedges of hornbeam and beds of 'Iceberg' roses. Tree damage near the aviary is the price paid for allowing brightly coloured macaws to fly free. Affected branches or trees are not removed as this would only spread the depredation further afield. Elsewhere, however, trees grow into fine specimens and conifers in particular create many picturesque groups.

West of the aviary is a slender metal pergola which was moved to its present position from the dairy garden, and below it the 'Tay Bridge'. The valley spanned by the bridge marks the route of a cable railway made to transport stone used for building the house from the now non-existent Westcott Railway Station. South of the aviary, fringed with varied conifers, is Daffodil Valley. To the east, beyond the open hillside below the terraces and concealed among evergreens, is a group of early eighteenth-century stone figures representing the four continents. These used to guard the main entrance to Waddesdon, which is no longer in use, but were moved to their present site in 1961.

Waddesdon was bequeathed to the National Trust by James de Rothschild in 1957. The aviary was opened in 1966 after extensive repairs and new trees and shrubs are planted every year to maintain as nearly as possible the original design and species in the garden.

Warren House, Bayford, Herts

---

2 acres; ½ gardener; gravel over clay. Open once in May and July for GS. Between Hertford (3 miles) and Hatfield (8 miles) S of B158.

Warren House is high in one corner of its garden, over which there are extensive rural views. A lawn below the house extends from a spreading cedar at one end to rose borders at the other, and beyond to the walled swimming-pool garden, tennis court and kitchen garden. These features are divided by a tall hawthorn hedge but the slope of the garden is such that there are extensive views over the hedge from the terrace.

The main path to the swimming pool garden turns to follow an herbaceous border then winds between roses and shrubs to the lower garden enclosed from surrounding fields *c*.1965. A large lawn narrows between a shrub border above and narrow herbaceous border below to terminate at an informal pool increasingly screened by a young Weeping Willow.

Although the garden in general is open, trees, walls and hedges enclose a variety of small borders in which bulbs, annuals, herbaceous plants and shrubs are displayed in more intimate surroundings. There are many interesting plants including some which are quite tender: *Hebe, Coronilla, Dimorphotheca* and *Cistus* for example.

Wasing Place, Aldermaston, Berks

5 acres in large park; 2 gardeners; soil mainly sandy. Open once in May, June and July for GS, NGS. 1 mile S of A4 midway between Reading and Newbury. Turn S off A4 at Woolhampton then left after one mile, or take A340 to Aldermaston then turn right.

Wasing Place is a varied and interesting garden pleasing not only for its large, mature trees and rhododendrons but for the evidence of much new planting testifying to the continuing enthusiasm of its owners and their two industrious gardeners.

The drive rises slowly through open parkland alternating with dense woodland, cool and enlivened with the sound of birds, to the eighteenth-century house. On the left is a walled kitchen garden concealed at a respectable distance from the house and, on the right, extensive views are obtained from the upper drive.

The kitchen garden is a delightful mixture of vegetables, fruit and flowers, the vegetables grown in rectangular plots surrounded by trained fruit which in turn frame borders of flowers. Flowering cherries overhang the border leading from the gate. Outside, by the early nineteenth-century 'American Border', a *Ginkgo* and an enormous cut-leaved beech are among the many interesting trees in the garden as a whole. The conservatory terminating the walks contains several climbing plants and two huge camellias one of which, 'Adolphe Audusson', has had its offspring widely planted in the main garden.

The main garden is, in contrast, quite irregular. The Victorian rhododendron clumps are being enriched with new planting. One has been hollowed to make a secluded camellia garden. Where old plants have fallen or died, hardy fuchsias, roses, hydrangeas and many other plants provide a long season of interest after bulbs and rhododendrons. Away from the house the planting thickens to enclose narrow paths and small clearings. *Halesia* and *Stewartia* have seeded, *Enkianthus, Azara, Kalmia* and *Pieris* have grown to large size while clematis and *Rosa filipes* 'Kiftsgate' climb through the support thus offered. Among the many large trees is a fine *Liquidambar styraciflua*. The atmosphere throughout is of well-loved, well-tended but casual luxuriance.

Waterperry Horticultural Centre, Wheatley, Oxon

83 acres, including 35 acres in cultivation and 8 acres garden; loam soil; 12 staff and up to 8 part-time workers. Gardens open twice each May and June, once in late July, Sept, Oct for GS, NGS and Church Fund. See HHCG. Nursery and gardens open Mon–Sat, 9–5, except holidays. 7 miles E of Oxford. Turn off A40 at Wheatley and follow signs.

Waterperry has long been known for training lady gardeners under the direction of Beatrice Havergal and Valerie Finnis. In 1971 the estate was acquired by the School for Economic Science but its function as a training centre continues. Students on weekend and summer courses are taught the elements of horticulture and help to maintain the garden. There remains a nucleus of experienced staff, advice is readily given and a wide range of plants is produced in the nursery, so Waterperry well merits the continued use of its title, 'Horticultural Centre'. Separate units of the nursery concentrate on fruit, intensive vegetable production, glasshouse crops, herbaceous and alpine plants.

The distinction between garden and nursery is not rigid. To the south and west of the house open lawns look out over farmland. To the east is the walled garden which accommodates glasshouses and alpine frames. The south-east quarter is the main area of cultivation, with frames, nursery rows of herbaceous plants, and the vegetable unit. Wide paths quartering this area are bordered by trained fruit, mainly cordon apples. It is in the wide strip between the walled garden and the vegetable unit that the main garden has been developed.

Against the south-facing wall is a long herbaceous border. With a small lawn bordered by irregular groups of shrubs and shaded by large trees it creates a surprisingly self-contained garden. At the west end of the lawn a curved border of old roses leads into the walled garden while, at the east end, the path dips into a rocky dell to a small bridge beyond which a grassy path continues to the River Thame. Winding paths between the shrubs lead out to a long rose border and an island bed of herbaceous plants between the garden itself and the nursery area beyond.

Another feature of the estate, although quite separate from the garden, is a Saxon church with fine stained glass, woodwork and brass.

Westfields, Oakley, Beds

2 acres; 1 gardener; calcareous clay soil. Open once in June for NGS. 4 miles N of Bedford, turn W off A6 to Oakley. At corner of High Street.

Westfields has an avenue of green and gold conifers alternating with green and purple broad-leaved trees throughout its $1\frac{1}{4}$ mile length. Nearer the house the canopy almost meets overhead then the drive turns between stone gateposts as if into another world.

The gentle west slope around the farmhouse has been developed since 1953, when Percy Cane was first consulted. The drive, with its broad grass verges meticulously maintained, leads by a small gate to the south terrace. This lateral entrance, with the main door of the house concealed by luxuriant planting, adds much to the charm of the design.

From the west terrace a long canal flanked by borders of paeony, lupin, floribunda rose and clipped lime draws the eye through wrought iron gates to the horizon. On the other side of the house, from the east lawn, vistas radiate north to a York stone paved rose garden, south across a lawn to more farmland views, and east to another gate on the skyline. From the top of the garden, a long walk follows the entire east and south boundaries shaded by cherries, laburnums and lilacs, returning to the south lawn and to the drive.

Within the rectangle enclosed by this walk, on the site of a former tennis court, is a rock garden with 150 tons of Westmorland limestone, a thatched summerhouse and a chain of pools leading down to a larger pool on the south lawn.

Across the drive is a walled garage court, a small salad garden and, through another heavy arched door, a transverse walk lined with shrub roses and bulbs. This walk leads, to the right, to the canal garden and, to the left, to the long drive back to Oakley.

The planting throughout is simple but generous, with much attention paid to winter appearance. Lawns, statuary, seats and gates add refinement to bold groups of *Genista hispanica*, Pfitzer Juniper and other evergreens. In 1976 Graham Thomas advised on the replanting of overgrown borders and the improvement has given the garden a new lease of life. The free planting and careful integration of its varied parts make the garden seem much larger than two acres and it is difficult to believe that it is all maintained by one young gardener.

Weston Gardens, Hitchin, Herts

A group of varied gardens on deep clay soil over chalk. Open once in June for GS. *Weston Park* also open in April for RC. 4 miles E of Letchworth exit from A1(M).

Gardens include:

Blakeney, 11 Munts Meadow ($\frac{1}{10}$ acre; no gardener): This is a new house with an open-plan front garden. The back garden, approximately 45 feet by 60 feet, faces south and the slight slope has been emphasized by low, curving walls. It is heavily planted with a tiny terrace, a sensibly open lawn partially concealed from the house by an island bed of roses, and a narrow walk between rose pillars and climber-clad fence on the west boundary.

The firm enclosure by fences, use of trees for height and shade, variety of spaces and freedom of planting combine to create a very charming garden.

Darnalls Hall (2 acres; part-time gardener): The large, flat lawn at Darnalls has roses in beds and on pillars around three sides, while the fourth is left open for views of the farm. A small herbaceous border screens the vegetable garden. In complete contrast to the general openness, however, a canal heavily shaded by native trees creates a cool, peaceful atmosphere around the boundary, ending as a more open pool near the entrance.

The farm buildings and livestock add further interest for the visitor.

Weston Lodge, Hall's Green (3 acres; part-time gardener): The garden at Weston Lodge has been developed around a loose cluster of farm buildings with many delightful effects. These range from a statuesque group of Giant Hogweed (*Heracleum mantegazzianum*) silhouetted against the black walls of a barn to the luxuriant growth of grape and Passion Flower on the walls of the house; from a double herbaceous border on the north-west side of the farmhouse to the kitchen garden on the south east. The herbaceous border has a carefully graded colour scheme while the kitchen garden, with box-edged gravel paths and blocks of fruit, vegetables and cut flowers is not without colour, especially when the alstroemerias are in flower.

The garden is not a compact and unified one. Instead it has been planned to take advantage of the various aspects and backgrounds. The deep shrub border at the end of the kitchen garden and the orchard on two sides of the main lawn serve not only their obvious primary purposes but provide shelter from the north and east, very necessary on this high and exposed site.

Weston Park (1 acre in large park; no gardener): Weston Park is essentially a Victorian garden. The house was much enlarged *c*.1870 and the garden was well stocked with shrubs and trees. *Zelkova, Fraxinus ornus* Manna Ash, *Davidia* Handkerchief or Ghost Tree and a huge *Arbutus menziesii* Madrone are among the interesting remnants beneath which a wild garden, carpeted with bulbs, has been made around the open lawn.

Recently, beech hedges enclosing twin herbaceous borders have been planted to provide a more colourful view from the drawing room and to shelter the small rose garden in this high and otherwise exposed garden. The conservatory is a further reminder of the garden's Victorian origins.

Westwell Manor, Westwell, Oxon

6 acres; 2 gardeners; limestone soil. Open twice each year for NGS. 2 miles SW of Burford. From A40 or A433 W of Burford, turn S; from A361 S of Burford, turn N through Holwell.

The garden was developed *c*.1900–1910 around a rambling assembly of Cotswold stone buildings and walls. The lines of the buildings have been extended with terrace walls, pergolas, paths and hedges to create a series of formal gardens decorated with bulbs, roses, herbaceous plants, climbers and topiary. The result is a charming, intimate and varied garden of the sort which only the Cotswolds seem able to produce.

The main drive arrives at the north forecourt between the house and tithe barn. South of the house two topiary yews frame herbaceous borders through the otherwise empty former kitchen garden. The present kitchen garden is through the cherry garden to the west. Long flower beds in which the topiary stands line the main path which passes a silver garden before descending steeply through a rose garden and pergola. This same path zig-zags along the hedge which screens the orchard to the south and east, passing a small rock garden to end at another, larger pergola.

A stream along the bottom of the garden widens into a secluded lily pool. Here the pergola also widens into a shaded arbour looking across a lawn to another shaded loggia converted from a cow shed. Raised borders above the formal garden thus contained accommodate more clipped yews which frame a vista across the back drive, beneath the tithe barn and into the north forecourt.

After more than half a century, the garden might be expected to assume a tired appearance but Westwell Manor has recently taken on a new lease of life following change of ownership and is likely to become even more attractive in the years ahead.

West Woodhay House, Newbury, Berks

---

16 acres inc. 3-acre kitchen garden; 2 gardeners; thin chalk soil. Open once in April for NGS. 6 miles SW of Newbury. From A4 turn S for Kintbury and continue for $2\frac{1}{2}$ miles; then follow signs to West Woodhay.

West Woodhay House, by Inigo Jones (1635), was reduced to its original size after the last war by the demolition of a large Victorian extension. It is sited high in the Downs with four quite different aspects, two of which command distant views.

To the north are the stables and services, well screened by trees and a wall. The walled forecourt to the east looks over a small lake to the 'new' church on the brow of the hill. The old drive may still be discerned in the field across the lake. To the south, the old churchyard and a woodland garden frame a view across the lawn to the Downs rising to nearly 1,000 feet. In contrast to this spaciousness, the west garden is heavily planted to create a more enclosed and sheltered area. The axis of the Garden Room (1960) extends to a rose garden and formal pool. Raised walks on either side meet in a small grove of beech. From the formal garden bordered by a yew walk, paths wind through the woodland garden between groups of rhododendrons, carpets of narcissi and golden-leaved trees.

Planting is broad in scale and varied in character from roses and herbaceous borders to the drifts of azaleas showing brilliantly against the shadowy woodland. Rhododendrons require careful cultivation in this high chalky garden but they receive generous peat mulches. The kitchen garden is quite separate from the pleasure gardens, opposite the main gates. Only half the area is now cultivated but new fruit trees have been planted and the greenhouses are used for commercial production of tomatoes and jasmine.

In all this is a remarkable garden, the more so when one considers that the house was virtually abandoned in 1931. Even as late as 1943 the drive was cut for hay, yet the garden has been reclaimed from scrub and young woodland by a staff never much larger than it is now.

West Wycombe Park, West Wycombe, Bucks (The National Trust)

55 acres; maintained without separate garden staff as part of large estate; thin soil over chalk. Open Easter Sun and Mon; Spring Bank Hol Sun and Mon; Mon–Fri in June; daily except Sat in July and Aug, 2.15–6. See HHCG. 3 miles W of High Wycombe on A40 at W end of West Wycombe.

West Wycombe was acquired by the Dashwood family in 1698 and the house begun *c*.1710. The major development of the house and its surroundings were by the 2nd Baronet Dashwood after his extensive tours in France, Germany, Italy, Greece, Russia and Asia Minor, tours which combined high living with serious scholarship. A founder member of the Dilettanti Society in 1732, Sir Francis himself created much of

West Wycombe, employing craftsmen to bring substance to his ideas.

The first phase, from 1739 to 1752, was probably the work of Morise Jolivet, with lodges, temples, a cascade and other features terminating formal vistas. Jolivet's survey of 1752, with its incomplete avenues and already irregular lake, shows the difficulties of attempting formality in this rolling terrain, and later developments adapted more easily to the increasing informality of the English landscape garden.

The house itself contributed to the scene to an unusual degree. The south colonnade and east portico were added *c.*1755 and in 1770/71 the west portico was made, modelled on the Temple of Bacchus at Telos. Carefully framed by trees, the house became, in effect, a series of garden temples rather than one house.

Between 1770 and 1781 Thomas Cook, reputedly a pupil of Lancelot Brown, added many new buildings designed by Revett, including the beautiful Music Temple on an island in the lake. In 1781 the estate passed to Sir John Dashwood-King who, in the mid-1790s, consulted Humphry Repton. Repton suggested simplifying some buildings and ordered much-needed thinning of the trees but his discerning advice offered in *Observations on the Theory and Practice of Landscape Gardening* has been more heeded in the twentieth century. West Wycombe escaped the lavish planting of exotics in the nineteenth century and was given to the National Trust in 1943 by Sir John Dashwood, 10th baronet, whose son Francis now occupies the house. Sir Francis Dashwood and the National Trust are removing over-large and over-mature trees to reduce the scale of the landscape and enhance reflections in the lake while carefully planting more trees to conceal twentieth-century intrusions, thus acting on Repton's advice to maintain and improve a gem of eighteenth-century landscape.

Wexham Springs, Stoke Poges, Bucks

70 acres (about 15 acres garden proper); 5–6 gardeners; soil varied, generally acid gravel over clay. Open twice in May for GS, NGS and once in late July for local horticultural societies. See HHCG. 2 miles N of Slough. From A4 turn N along Wexham Road in Slough (between Station and A412 roundabout); from A40 turn S at 'French Horn' to Fulmer, then 1 mile along Framewood Road.

Wexham Springs is of two distinct ages. The house was built in 1860 and enlarged in 1892 for Col. L.H. Hanbury, a keen horticulturist, and many fine trees and shrubs remain, especially in the woodland south of the house. In 1946 the property was acquired by the Cement and Concrete Association for development as a research station. The Association, working with several distinguished architects and landscape architects, has developed new gardens as well as maintaining much of the old.

One objective of the new gardens is to demonstrate the versatility of concrete. In this they succeed admirably not only in the wide range of concrete finishes and garden features, but in the associated planting. A wide terrace south of the house is furnished with grey-leaved and herbaceous plants. Concrete arches spanning the main path are planted alternately with honeysuckle and clematis. (The success of the clematis on the north side of the arches lends support to the tradition of shading their roots!) The walk continues west of the house to display panels of wall and paving finishes. In the other direction a York-paved rose garden and long two-toned path bordered by lavender lead to the Meynell Building.

From the lawn and rose garden, paths cross and re-cross a stream through the rock garden, into an old rhododendron glade among redwoods and maples. Large specimens of many unusual plants occur along the paths: *Magnolia obovata, Cornus florida* 'Rubra', an enormous *Cryptomeria japonica* 'Elegans' and the rare *Stewartia malacodendron* are but a few. The looped path opens to the west by a small lake ringed with trees including two *Taxodium distichum* displaying their characteristic 'knees'.

South of the Meynell Building is a garden designed by Sylvia Crowe. A sophisticated paved court with bold foliage plants is linked to pools of beautifully finished concrete. This marks the end of the garden proper but the rest of the estate has excellent examples of design and planting. Courtyards, block walls in the car parks and a Horse Chestnut avenue along the 'Philosophers' Walk' are worth inspection. Half way along the Walk is a long storage building, the north side of which, overlooking playing fields, has four large arbours separated by flourishing borders of shade-tolerant shrubs and climbers, a planting design by Susan Jellicoe. Philosophers' Walk connects Wexham Springs to Fulmer Grange, the training centre of the Cement and Concrete Association. A sunken rose garden and a water lily canal provide a suitable setting for the old house (1911) while the newer buildings have a simpler setting of shade trees and grass.

White Cottage, Shepherd's Green, Oxon

$\frac{3}{4}$ acre; no gardener; patchy clay and acid sand over chalk. Open once in June for GS. Plant sales. (See also *Fishers*, which is adjacent.) 4 miles W of Henley-on-Thames, via road to Rotherfield Greys, bear right after village green.

The original garden was extended to its present size in 1969 and has been developed mainly since then. Many plants are raised from cuttings and most are labelled.

North of the house are heathers, low conifers and a flourishing 'fedge' of ivy with old roses to frame the entrance. South of the house is a very sheltered corner. Originally containing only four rose beds, this corner has been enriched with grey-leaved and pastel-flowered plants and with innumerable crevice plants, so it is never without interest. A box hedge surrounds the corner, clipped at strategic points into three plump birds, one of which appropriately houses a wren's nest.

A low yew hedge extends across the garden to the vegetable plot. Both sides of the hedge have borders: paeonies, rodgersias, ferns and hardy arum lilies on the shady side; roses, potentillas and herbaceous plants, especially delphiniums, on the south. Across the shallow channel marking the old boundary are informal shrub beds, one with evergreens and other good foliage plants.

Although the garden is divided into six parts, they open naturally one into another. The planting is free and repeated, resulting in a harmonious garden of considerable charm.

White Horse, Finchampstead, Berks

6 acres; 1 gardener; sandy soil. Open every day for charities, including GS, NGS. 8 miles SE of Reading, 4 miles S of Wokingham by Finchamstead church. Garden signposted from B3016, B3348.

White Horse garden is open for many charities but especially for maintenance of the church which can be seen from the upper level of the garden. It has been developed since 1950 and now covers about six acres, with an open level area at the top and thickly planted steep slopes.

A gate beside the house leads to a long lawn bordered with stone troughs and dwarf conifers. Beyond the lawn is a series of small paved rectangular gardens on the sites of demolished greenhouses. There are rose gardens, a cactus garden, fish ponds and everywhere attractive pots, old paving materials and luxuriant plants. The one remaining greenhouse is used for propagating in spring and later for display.

From the house a narrow opening leads down to the main lawn. An island bed of *Peltiphyllum*, *Astilbe* and other waterside plants belies the sandy soil, but this bed is polythene lined as is the small pool across the lawn. Well-stocked borders surround the lawn and almost conceal the path which begins by the pool as a small extension to the lawn, dividing to form three paths. Two branch, wind and make their way by level stretches and steps to the bottom of the garden while the third follows a level route just below the paved gardens under a young Deodar to a grass slope with fine views.

It is pointless to try to describe the planting in any detail. Suffice it to say that on the steep slope there are two slight spurs and a valley, densely planted and interlaced with narrow paths. Conifers on the upper slope emphasize the valley from some points and tower against the sky despite their relatively small size. Elsewhere shrub roses, dahlias, fuchsias, colchicums, spring bulbs, heathers and many other plants ensure that there is always something to see, and although the steep slopes are inaccessible to wheelchairs there is much to be seen from the upper part of the garden. The entrance fee is very small but one should not be deterred by thinking that this indicates interest of similar proportions!

Wilcote House, near Finstock, Oxon

6 acres; 1 gardener plus part-time help; soil heavy calcareous loam mainly lost beneath old buildings. Open once in May/June for NGS. Midway between Witney and Woodstock, 2 miles N of Northleigh on road to Finstock, just N of Wilcote crossroads.

There can be few other gardens in which the house plays such an important part in garden views. The Jacobean and Queen Anne house was greatly enlarged in 1860 and the drive now passes through three courtyards of very different characters between the lime avenue at the entrance and the main garden south and east of the house.

The first court is heavily planted, with sunny corners for *Crinum, Ceanothus* and *Cytisus battandieri* and shady areas for hostas and hydrangeas. The second is small, high walled and sparsely planted while the third is open with narrow borders of lavender and bergenia. The terraced lawn south of the house continues along the east side to a small garden of rugosa roses then steps down between beech hedges to the tennis court and a stone summerhouse.

The main lines of the garden, the lime avenue and beech hedges were established from 1938, mainly after 1944. The present owners, capitalizing on great expanses of wall of every aspect and height, have introduced a wide range of climbers since 1972. They are also experimenting with colour groupings of trees, shrubs and lower plants appropriate to the various situations, and there is no doubt that the garden of Wilcote House will go from strength to strength for many years.

Wilcote Manor, Near Finstock, Oxon

4½ acres; part-time help; soil, limestone brash. Open once in April for NGS (church also open). Directions as for Wilcote House but take turning to Ramsden from Wilcote crossroads.

The garden of Wilcote Manor, formerly a narrow strip around the attractive Elizabethan house, was enlarged in 1937 to include the adjacent field and two fine oaks, reputed to be nearly 1,000 years old. The oaks were brought into the garden visually by extending twin yew hedges out, around and beyond them to create a long vista terminated by shapely Sweet Gums. One of these lost the largest of its three main branches early in 1975 but it was successfully winched back into place.

Other yews, formerly used to screen the kitchens, are topped with strange topiary animals. The four corners of the garden are occupied by orchards, vegetables and small rose garden, concealed by the hedges and four long borders flanking the vista.

Originally planted as a spring garden, the garden is still particularly beautiful in this season with magnolias and amelanchiers in the borders and bulbs in the grass. The present owners have been refurbishing the borders gradually since 1973 to extend the season of interest and are creating not only a garden of increasing beauty but a fine example of what can be achieved on a large flat site with very little help.

Windsor Great Park, Windsor, Berks (The Crown Estate)

See also *Frogmore Gardens* which is in the Home Park.

Begun in the eleventh century, Windsor Great Park was largely formed by 1365. In addition to its extensive natural forests, innumerable other trees, native and exotic have been planted since 1580. In 1746, William, Duke of Cumberland began the deliberate landscaping of the Park, using his troops recently returned from the Battle of

Culloden to dig Virginia Water and the various smaller ponds which keep the 130-acre main lake free of silt.

The whole of Windsor is rich in history, not least the great castle surmounting the steep chalk outcrop on the northern edge, but the main area of interest to gardeners lies to the south where two of England's finest gardens, the *Savill* and *Valley Gardens*, have been formed in this century on the deep, acid Bagshot sand which overlies the London clay found elsewhere in the Park. 12 student gardeners are trained and employed in the gardens in addition to the permanent staff.

Savill Garden

> 35 acres; 10 gardeners; acid sand. Open daily, March–Oct, 10–6 (7 pm in summer). Plant sales. From A30 turn NW at signpost between A328 (Englefield Green) and A329 (Sunningdale) into Wick Road then left at end into Wick Lane.

Savill Garden began in 1932 as a small bog garden and grew under the direction of Sir Eric Savill until, by 1939, the perimeter was well established. From 1950 the central part was developed on more formal lines. Planting and replanting has continued to the present day for the policy is to keep plantings young and vigorous. In 1976 the west boundary was extended to include a corner which will be planted particularly for autumn colour.

Savill was formed as a woodland garden, some distance from any buildings. The addition of a restaurant in 1963, therefore, provided not only a new amenity but the focus for a new area, more architectural and intimate in character than the garden as a whole. From the restaurant is one of the finest views in the garden, across ponds and grassy clearings fringed with rhododendrons to the main expanse of the Park beyond. On the slope south of the restaurant is a fine stand of beech carpeted with silvery moss, respected and untrampled by the thousands of visitors who come each year. Below are the peat beds developed in recent years to provide a congenial home for the most difficult woodland plants. In 1977 a bridge was constructed across the nearby pond to mark HM the Queen's Silver Jubilee.

Above the bridge, the stream is bordered by wide drifts of primulas, *Meconopsis*, lilies, ferns and other waterside plants merging imperceptibly into the rhododendrons and related shrubs which give shape to informal glades and rides with which the woodland is intersected. On higher ground to the west, less prone to spring frosts, magnolias and camellias are planted in great variety on either side of the main ride sloping down again to rhododendrons along the north boundary. Plants are not segregated into tight botanical groupings but are used with great discrimination beneath a canopy of forest trees, forming in themselves a lower canopy for carpets of many woodland flowers and ferns.

In the north-east corner the post-war garden creates quite a different note. The main lawn within the rhododendrons emerges between magnificent herbaceous borders over 100 yards in length. On either side are rose gardens: to the south are shrub roses and the horseshoe border; to the north, surrounded by a hedge of *Chamaecyparis lawsoniana* are hybrid tea roses. The high buttressed wall beyond the hedges was built in 1950 with bricks from the bombed houses of West Ham. Until the restaurant was built, this was the only wall in the garden and it still provides support for several wall plants. At its foot are raised beds with a variety of soil mixes providing ideal habitats for a wide range of bulbs and alpines: an excellent model for gardeners wishing to grow alpines where a rockery would be incongruous.

Below the herbaceous borders, the Temperate House accommodates tender rhododendrons and other plants requiring similar conditions. The Weeping Willow nearby was the first tree to be put in the garden, and from it one can follow the winding stream edged with ferns, *Rodgersia, Lysichitum, Primula, Iris* and a host of other plants back to the main ride, restaurant and plantsman's corner, where a wide selection of plants can be purchased.

The Valley Gardens

300 acres; 18 gardeners; acid sand. Open every day, sunrise to sunset. Car parks near the junction of A30 and A329 (Wheatsheaf Hotel) and at Wick Road (see Savill, above) are 1 mile from the gardens. A car park adjacent to the Valley Gardens is open daily. Apr–Jun for which a charge is made. Entrance to car park is at junction of Wick Road and Wick Lane.

The Valley Gardens tend to be thought of as a rhododendron collection to be visited in May or June. In fact the rhododendron season alone extends from December for early flowering species to August for such late hybrids as 'Redcap' and 'Polar Bear' with interest of foliage all the year, and recent plantings of hydrangeas, camellias, heathers, magnolias and trees for flower and autumn colour ensure that the gardens are never without considerable interest. Even before this diversification there was not only a rhododendron *collection* of international renown but a rhododendron *garden* arranged by a discriminating gardener on a series of undulations sloping southwards to the edge of Virginia Water. There are high vantage points to the north, overlooking heavily planted slopes, with grass rides winding down to vistas of the lake.

The Pinetum was established in 1935 before the Valley Garden proper. It provides much winter interest but the *Metasequoia* grove must be its most notable feature. *Metasequoia glyptostroboides*, the Dawn Redwood, has flourished in cultivation since its discovery in 1946/7 and many gardeners boast a specimen, but here are about 200 specimens, the smaller ones propagated from an original group which were among the first to be planted in Britain.

Pinetum Valley is more-or-less central in the Valley Gardens collectively. To the west is the Hydrangea Garden, begun in 1963/4 and the older *Rhododendron* species collection which took four years to move here from Tower Court, Ascot after the death of J.B. Stevenson in 1951. He had spent 50 years amassing the collection, which has continued to increase in its new situation. East of the Pinetum is the Heather Garden, developed since 1954 and cleverly exploiting the hummocky terrain and natural plant communities of this pre-1918 gravel-pit. To the south is the Valley Garden proper with two valleys of azaleas and rhododendrons curving down to Virginia Water.

On the eastern edge of the Valley Garden are camellias and the famous Punch Bowl where massed ranks of evergreen azaleas create a flamboyant scene to which thousands of visitors flock each year. Although a car park is opened especially for the peak season the rest of the year offers many other examples of flowers, foliage and plant form as well as quieter conditions in which to appreciate them.

Woburn Abbey, Woburn, Beds (Trustees of the Bedford Estates)

---

42 acres in 3,000-acre park; 3 gardeners plus 3 part-time; soil varies from clay to pure sand. Park open late Mar–Aug, 10.30–5 (Suns, 10–5.30); Sept–late Oct, 11–4.30 (Suns, 11–5); late Oct–late Mar, 11–3.30 every day. Abbey open late Mar–late Oct from 11.30; late Oct–late Mar, from 1 pm. See HHCG. In Woburn, 8½ miles NW of Dunstable.

Although Woburn was the last of England's great houses to open to the public, it is today probably the best known. Woburn is designed on a grand scale: the house, twin stable blocks and intervening court alone cover five acres and the surroundings are more appropriately described as parkland than gardens.

The private garden south of the house is formal and simple with gravel walks, urns, statues and occasional flower beds. To the east the garden is less regular with a Chinese pavilion in the centre of a small maze as its most charming feature.

The park itself is not without horticultural interest. Even before the 4th Duke rebuilt the house in 1750, he planted many evergreen oaks, cedars and other trees. The 5th Duke continued his grandfather's interest in farming, tree planting and remodelling houses, and under the 6th Duke, Woburn became famous for its many rare trees. A redwood avenue can still be seen from the cable car but other plants have been lost in the undergrowth. In 1804 Repton prepared a scheme for the park, as a result of which the lake was made less formal and several picturesque cottage retreats were built in the park.

Later in the nineteenth century interest turned from plants to animals. Both the 10th and 11th Dukes had large collections of birds and mammals, the rarest being the herd of Père David deer. These animals formed a natural foundation for the Wild Animal Kingdom which, with the Abbey and its magnificent contents, form the nucleus of many attractions developed at Woburn since the 13th Duke, faced with £5½ million in death duties, decided to open his house to the public in 1955.

Woodhall Park, Watton-at-Stone, Herts

2 acres; no gardener; gravel over clay. Open once in June for NGS. Entrance on W side of A602 between Hertford (5 miles) and Watton-at-Stone (1 mile).

The main house at Woodhall Park was abandoned in 1934 (it is now Heathmount School), but in 1957/8 the eighteenth-century stables were converted into a house and two cottages. The garden was planned by Brenda Colvin but the choice of plants is that of its owners.

From the entrance, enclosed by beech hedges, a vista extends through the arches of the stable-yard and between long herbaceous borders. One border conceals the kitchen garden while the other is deepened with shrubs to surround the elliptical garden of the loggia on the west end of the house. The open grass beyond has a path mown through the new conifer planting at the far west end.

The main south front of the house has an elegant terrace below which the cross slope has been levelled and a steep bank and ha-ha constructed to form a horseshoe-shaped ridge enclosing a lawn well proportioned to set off a fine copper beech. A narrow path around the summit of the ridge gives interesting views inwards to the house and out over the park through the now overgrown shrubs which clothe the banks.

Woolleys, Hambleden, Bucks

3 acres; 1 gardener; thin chalk soil. Open once in April for NGS. 4 miles NE of Henley-on-Thames on N edge of Hambleden. 1 mile N of A4155 (Henley–Marlow).

Woolleys might well serve as a text-book example of a characteristic chalk garden. Hedges of beech, hazel, yew and box and an old flint wall divide the garden into various compartments and most of the garden is grass, rich in chalkland wild flowers and bulbs.

The big Horse Chestnut south of the house has a carpet of Winter Aconite and anemones. The south boundary is open with a few large beech in long grass, and primrose, crocus, narcissus, bluebell and tulip beneath. West of the house the lawn has been levelled and enclosed by informal banks. Steep, irregular mounds of spoil behind the flint wall effectively conceal curving shrub borders and the orchard beyond. Again the mounds are thickly planted with narcissus.

Climbing roses concealing the tennis court also clothe the arch leading to the old vegetable garden, of which nothing remains except the sentinel fruit trees bordering the cross-paths. The present, smaller vegetable garden is reached from the orchard beneath an enormous hazel. Borders of iris, paeonies and roses edged with catmint create a charming picture along the vegetable garden paths leading back to the main lawn.

Wrest Park, Silsoe, Beds (Department of the Environment)

80 acres; 6 gardeners; clay soil. Open Sat, Sun and Bank Hols (not Good Friday). April 10–5.30, May–Sept 10–7. See HHCG. E of A6 between Luton (10 miles) and Bedford (10 miles).

Nikolaus Pevsner described the present house, built in 1834–9 as unique in England for its consistent adherence to the French Renaissance style. This consistency extends to the garden, ideally suited to the flat landscape of the area. The vista, across the parterre to the distant reflection of Archer's pavilion in the Long Water creates an immediate impression of magnificence. As in the Renaissance gardens themselves, however, the unity of the whole reveals, on closer inspection, great variety in the parts.

The gardens were begun in 1706 by the 12th Earl of Kent (created 1st Duke of Kent in 1710) and developed throughout his life as a formal woodland dissected by long rides terminated by eye-catchers. The woods flanked the broad central vista with its central canal terminated by a domed pavilion designed by Thomas Archer in 1709–11. The Duke died in 1740. From 1758–60 his grand-daughter Jemima Campbell and her husband Philip Yorke, 2nd Earl of Hardwicke commissioned Lancelot Brown to alter the gardens. Fortunately Brown's alterations – winding rides through the woods and the serpentine river which now encompasses the garden – were made without destroying the original scheme.

The Manor passed in turn to the eldest daughter and, in 1833, to her nephew Thomas Philip, 2nd Earl de Grey. Thomas was encouraged by his aunt to pursue his interest in art and architecture. Within a year of his inheritance the first stone was laid for a new, convenient and large house, north of the old house which he demolished. Much of the design was by the 2nd Earl with the help of his architectural assistant Clephane, who may have designed the Orangery. The great walled garden was added in 1836 and many statues were brought later from the Great Exhibition of 1851. The Chinese Bridge crossing Brown's river south east of the house was added in 1874 and is the third of its genre. It formed part of an oriental garden made around it.

The garden also has much of horticultural interest. The entrance, through the Strangers' Gate, is into a rose garden between the large conservatory and the walled garden. Long herbaceous and shrub borders half conceal the walled garden, within the walls of which there are greenhouses, fruit cages and splendid wall plants including a Judas Tree (*Cercis siliquastrum*) and one of the oldest wisterias in the country, spanning over 100 feet of wall.

Wroxton College, Banbury, Oxon

---

64 acres; 2 gardeners; stony soil over clay. Open one weekend in May for NGS. 4 miles W of Banbury on A422 (Banbury–Stratford) in village of Wroxton.

The gardens of Wroxton Abbey, as the College was known prior to its acquisition by Fairleigh Dickinson University in 1964, are of considerable historical interest and enough remains of the great terrace, the lakes and fine trees to make an interesting visit.

An Augustinian priory from 1217 to 1537, the house was rebuilt by 1618 of the local Hornton stone, and was, for three centuries, occupied by the North family. Early in the eighteenth century Tilleman Bobart designed a garden in the French manner, with a long canal, octagonal basin, great terrace and parterre. The terrace with its cross-walk and cedars remains but other features disappeared when, from 1733, Francis North, 1st Earl of Guilford began making a garden in the new picturesque or naturalist manner. Lawn replaced the parterre and, with help from Sanderson Miller, formal waters were turned into a series of lakes, with woods and winding walks enlivened by Chinese and gothic buildings. The flimsier buildings quickly vanished but several stone buildings, the lakes and many walks remain of interest to the historian, gardener and naturalist: the woods, lake margins, old trees and ancient lawns are rich in wildlife.

Youngsbury, Wadesmill, Herts

12 acres; 1 gardener; gravel soil overlying clay. Open once in June for NGS or RC etc. 2½ miles N of Ware on A10 at Wadesmill.

Youngsbury is an eighteenth-century house around an older core. The south terrace looks over a shrub border and open lawn, across a ha-ha to the park. The lake, the main feature of Lancelot Brown's design for the park, is now narrowed to a small river but greener than average crops in the surrounding field mark its original outline. The terrace itself, attractively planted when the garden was revised in 1963/4 extends beyond the house to a weeping silver pear against older yew hedges. *Hebe* and *Euphorbia* shelter against the house while grey leaved rue, *Ballota*, and *Senecio* 'Sunshine' (*greyii*) lap over the terrace wall to join with shrubs in the border beneath. Thymes, *Alchemilla* and *Stachys* have seeded freely into the terrace.

East of the house is open lawn with a few large trees: yews to conceal the back of the house, cedar and beech to mark the approach to a small woodland walk.

North of the house is the Elizabethan walled garden, where most of the gardening effort is now concentrated. The outer walls have curved borders in which yellow-flowered shrubs predominate, with magnolias and crab apples for earlier flower. Within the gate the yellow theme continues with grey and golden foliage backed by shrub roses in deep double borders, terminating at a raised seat from which the scent and foliage of *Cytisus battandieri* on the wall can be appreciated at close range. Behind the borders are new fruit plantings, a small orchard of flowering cherries and crab apples and in the south-west corner a dilapidated but delightful rustic shelter, its tiled roof lined with a mosaic of pine and larch cones.

Index